ACCENTS ON OPERA

A SERIES OF BRIEF ESSAYS

STRESSING KNOWN AND LITTLE KNOWN

FACTS AND FACETS OF A FAMILIAR ART

By BORIS GOLDOVSKY

WITH VITAL STATISTICS ON OPERATIC PREMIÈRES

BY MARY ELLIS PELTZ

SPONSORED BY

THE METROPOLITAN OPERA GUILD, Inc.
NEW YORK

Essay Index Reprint Series

 BOOKS FOR LIBRARIES PRESS
FREEPORT, NEW YORK

TWELVE minutes for a glimpse of opera background during one intermission of the Metropolitan Opera Broadcasts! Such has been the opportunity afforded me by the Texas Company during the past eight seasons. The challenge has been an exciting one! Twelve minutes—plus a moment or two of illustrations at the piano—to bring some fresh aspect of opera to millions of opera listeners. Under the circumstances each discussion could deal with only one or two topics, carefully chosen from my own store of enthusiasms to deepen the enjoyment of the average listener.

The results, gratifying in themselves, have prompted me to offer a collection of these accents, in book form, to opera lovers everywhere. First there has been the mail from the radio audience, indicating keen interest in the program, "Opera News on the Air." Then there has been the response from The Metropolitan Opera Guild whose Publications Director, Mrs. John DeWitt Peltz, reorganized and revised the original broadcast scripts as brief articles in the Guild magazine, *Opera News*. And finally there is the conviction, born of my own experience both as producer and teacher in the field of opera, that it is in the byways and corners of the art, its relation to history, literature, painting, its technical aspects as well as its human frailties and fancies that the average layman finds his first happy contacts. The producers of the intermission broadcasts gave me a reasonably free hand to introduce any operatic topic which fascinated me personally, provided that it was not too technical and that we could make it sufficiently exciting and entertaining to our listeners. As a result the reader can expect to find in these pages anything from the lighting problems of Mozart's day to Schopenhauer's philosophy of ethics; from the unpublished pages of "Carmen" to Rossini's fondness for fresh bologna sausages.

I cannot conclude this brief introduction without a word of appreciation to the Metropolitan Opera, whose broadcasts have brought the art of opera into the American way of life; to the Texas Company, generous sponsors of the broadcasts, who provided a vehicle for my ideas as an intermission feature; to Henry Souvaine and his associates, producers of the Metropolitan Opera Broadcasts, including this program; to many colleagues who have assisted me in the preparation of the script; and to the various artists who appeared on the air with me, adding the charm of their personalities and a generous measure of their knowledge and experience. Above all my appreciation goes to the opera public, whose discerning enthusiasm has inspired me to offer these brief essays on opera in the hope that they may accent new details of enjoyment in the art which has brought us together.

BORIS GOLDOVSKY

CONTENTS

All photographs are by SEDGE LEBLANG, official METROPOLITAN OPERA HOUSE photographer, and may be found following page 152.

ACCENTS ON OPERA

AÏDA

I F Giuseppe Verdi had had the misfortune, like Schubert or Mozart, to die at an early age, his name, unlike those of the other two masters, would survive today only in the records of a few scholarly students of Italian opera.

It was only when Verdi was well past the age of thirty-five that he began to write the music for which he is now remembered, while his early works, such as "Oberto" and "Nabucco" hardly suggest the composer of "Otello" and "Falstaff." "Rigoletto," the earliest of his works to have remained in the standard repertory, was actually his fifteenth stage composition and by no means a youthful effort. By the time he had reached "Aïda," at the age of fifty-seven, Verdi had achieved absolute mastery of both the musical and theatrical elements of his art.

This drama of love, jealousy, duty, and sacrifice is undoubtedly one of the most successful and most beloved operas ever written. Its melodies and its story have probably become everywhere more popular than any of the composer's other works. Why is that so? What makes the heart of every listener beat faster as he follows Radames and Aïda through their tragic love? The music, of course, provides a breath-taking succession of immortal melodies, but that alone does not explain the deep emotional impact of the opera and the success which has electrified audiences from the first hearing of the opera on Christmas Eve, 1871.

It is the sincerity and urgency of its utterance which give this work its passionate vitality and irresistible appeal. Verdi himself is responsible for making his characters such strong, powerful

3

personalities on the stage. He was the spark plug in making the libretto so effective, as we are able to observe from the long and detailed correspondence between Verdi and his poet-text-writer, Antonio Ghislanzoni. When the libretto of "Aïda" was being hammered into final shape, the writer, for some reason unknown to us, was unable to join the composer. Thus, what would have otherwise occurred in conversation and been lost forever to posterity, has luckily been put down in a series of fascinating letters between the two men. This correspondence makes one thing very clear: Verdi was fanatically determined to make human beings out of what could easily have become operatic puppets. He battles for every word, every detail.

One example offers especially striking proof of Verdi's infallible dramatic instinct. It occurs in the great second-act duet between Amneris and Aïda, where Amneris at last tricks Aïda into disclosing the secret of her unhapy love. Just before the end of this duet, Ghislanzoni submitted the following lines to Verdi:

I love him also, do you hear?
I love him, hear and tremble!
You are my rival, that is clear;
It's useless to dissemble!

Verdi brushed aside these pompous words. "Abandon rhyme, rhythm, stanza," he commands the writer. "Forget it all!" Thus, instead of the polished verses of the poet, we now find at this place Verdi's violent prose: "Yes, you love him, but so do I! Do you hear me? I am your rival! I, the daughter of the Pharaohs!"

In these letters, Verdi comments repeatedly on what he calls *"la parola scenica,"* or "the dramatic word." As used by Verdi, it means the only expression that really fits the situation, the word that comes from the heart. He fought hard for this *"parola scenica."*

In the third-act duet between Amonasro and Aïda, father and daughter, Ghislanzoni submitted one phrase which excited Verdi and struck fire in his mind. It was: "*O patria, quanto mi costi!*" "Oh fatherland, how much you cost me!" "This sentence must be preserved," he wrote Ghislanzoni. Unfortunately for the librettist, Verdi did not favor the rest of the scene. He objected particularly to the section following the duet between Amonasro and Aïda, where the father rejects his daughter and crushes her with words that fall horribly on her ears: "You are not my daughter, you are the slave of the Egyptians." This was to be followed, according to Ghislanzoni's draft, by the customary *cabaletta,* a short, fast, closing section which was the usual windup for a duet or an aria of the period. But Verdi said, "No *cabalettas* here! In her state of terror and moral depression, Aïda cannot possibly sing an extended melodic passage. Just give me a few broken words which she can utter *con voce cupa,* in a low, hollow voice." The result we all know.

Disregarding meter, disregarding all the rules of the poet, Verdi wrote some of his greatest musical passages.

In the fourth-act duet between Amneris and Radames, Verdi himself was surprised that he had succeeded in finding an appropriate melody to words which seemed to him like the phrases of a jurist. Amneris pleads with Radames as a lawyer would plead with his client. First, she tries to control herself, tries to be objective—there is still hope! But at the end of each sentence the fire that burns in her heart breaks out, until at last the score commands her to sing *con agitazione, animando, con espressione,* as she intones her final passionate, futile plea.

In connection with this scene, Verdi made a revealing statement to Ghislanzoni. "Under these words of a lawyer," he wrote, "there beats the heart of a woman, desperate with ardent love. Only music can depict what goes on in her soul, hidden behind her words."

This is the unique magic of opera: the beating of the human heart behind the spoken word. In the case of "Aïda," this mastery of humanization appears particularly remarkable. In its basic idea and its setting against a background of war, processions, religious ceremonies, trials, and death, the opera could easily have become a blood-and-thunder spectacle in the style of so many old-fashioned grand operas of the time. Verdi, however, refused to limit himself to a superficial picture of battles and processions in ancient Egypt. He was not content with ballets, warriors, elephants, and marches with cymbals and drums. All this is in "Aïda," of course, but the astonishing impact of the work is the result of the pulsing life of human beings, which far surpasses in its power and grandeur the marching feet of the soldiers, the hollow sound of the fanfares, and the mighty echo that is reflected from the walls of the temple of Phtha. The walls of the temple may crumble, and all the power of Phtha may be swept away in the dust, but the human heart beats on. Its passions are timeless and ageless. This is the secret of "Aïda's" magic and eternal youth.

Giuseppe Verdi (1813-1901) consented to compose the music to the story of "Aïda" in early 1870, encouraged by the effectiveness of a plot submitted to him by his friend Camille du Locle

(1832-1903). This plot was the invention of a French Egyptologist, Mariette Bey, who had been sent to Cairo in 1850 by the Louvre authorities in Paris. The author of the libretto was Antonio Ghislanzoni (1824-1893), who worked in close collaboration with the composer through the summer of 1870. The Cairo première, for which the Khedive, Draneht Bey, had commissioned the opera, was delayed by the Franco-Prussian War. It was followed by the Milan production of February 8, 1872.

Little is known of the artists responsible for the world première at Cairo on Christmas Eve, 1871. We learn that the conductor, Giovanni Bottesini, was disturbed by the applause which interrupted the action. The singers are little more than names: Antonietta Anastasi-Pozzoni was Aïda; Eleonora Grossi, Amneris; Pietro Mongini, Radames; Francesco Steller, Amonasro; Paolo Medini, Ramfis; Tommaso Costa, the King, and Stecchie Bottardi, the Messenger.

When Max Strakosch first brought "Aïda" to America on November 26, 1873, he entrusted the baton to Emanuele Muzio, whom Verdi had sent to Cairo as his personal emissary for the première. Two hundred performers gathered on the stage of the Academy of Music for the triumph scene, and a capacity audience gave "hearty applause" to Ottavia Torriani, the Aïda. Annie Louise Cary, the renowned contralto from Maine, was commended for her "passion and power" as an actress by the New York Times. Victor Maurel, twenty-five years old but already famous, sang Amonasro, while Italo Campanini, only two years his senior, was the Radames. Scolari was the King and Giovanni Boy the Messenger.

German was the language for "Aïda's" first performance at the Metropolitan Opera House, November 12, 1886, under Anton Seidl's baton. The Aïda was Therese Foerster, prima donna of the Court Theater in Vienna. She was the wife of

Victor Herbert, soon to become first 'cellist in the Metropolitan Opera orchestra. Marianne Brandt, the first Metropolitan Fidelio and one of the first Bayreuth Kundrys, sang Amneris. Carl Zobel was Radames and Adolf Robinson was Amonasro. The Ramfis was Emil Fischer, remembered as the first and one of the greatest protagonists of Hans Sachs at the Metropolitan. George Sieglitz was the King and Otto Kemlitz the Messenger. "In the labors of almost all the artists there was discerned a want of refinement in feeling and expression," wrote W. J. Henderson in the Times, stressing the need for another cast to present Italian opera.

THE BARBER OF SEVILLE

STRANGE as it may seem to us today, there was a whole generation of music lovers, from the 1820's to the 1840's, for whom Gioacchino Rossini was the undisputed king of composers, living or dead. It is difficult for us even to imagine the idolatry which was lavished upon Rossini. In the eyes of the opera lovers of his time, he towered head and shoulders above a mere Mozart, Gluck, or Beethoven!

The conventional picture of the composer, neglected by his contemporaries and starving in a garret, hardly fits Rossini. Few composers ever enjoyed such success within their own lifetime.

The reason for Rossini's enormous vogue is readily apparent. His music is fresh, gay, simple, easily understood at first hearing, and certainly not the sort of art that must wait for succeeding generations to discover its underlying significance. His melodies bubble forth from a seemingly inexhaustible source of gaiety and *joie de vivre*, and the composer sits on top of the world, pleasantly intoxicated with his own success. No wonder listeners of a hundred and thirty years ago were swept away by it. Even today "Rossini 1816" remains a great vintage wine! It hasn't soured or grown flat; if anything, it has improved with age, as a good wine should. What could be more irresistible than the sheer gaiety of the barber's description of his emporium in the duet with the Count at the end of the first act?

10

Has there ever been a more rollicking piece written than the "Largo al factotum," as Figaro cries: "Make way!"

This same sparkle also permeates such ensembles as the finale of the last act, which celebrates the overcoming of the obstacles that threatened the happiness of the young couple. Love has triumphed and gaiety is the order of the day.

11

FINALE. ALLEGRO

It has often been asked why Rossini, who had such an enormous reputation in his own day, suddenly stopped composing in the middle of a life devoted to feverish productivity. As a teacher of mine once put it: Rossini wrote thirty-eight operas in the first thirty-eight years of his life. Then he lived another thirty-eight years in which he wrote none.

One possible explanation of this strange circumstance is that Rossini enjoyed his creature comforts and good times much more than he enjoyed working. So he stopped working!

To be sure, there was an element of disappointment in his career. His very last opera, "William Tell," for which he had great hopes, never enjoyed an unqualified success, and Rossini lived to see his fame overshadowed by Meyerbeer, Halévy, and others. I am convinced that even though "William Tell" had something to do with his early retirement, Rossini's love of the good things of life was a more potent factor.

Rossini had a tremendous reputation as a gourmet and was himself a fine cook. In fact, his passion for food provides one clue for a bit of musical detective work. In studying Rossini's scores, one notices that in many instances the second oboe player is scored for at the very beginning of the opera and not again until the very end of the first act. Otherwise the second oboe player is completely silent, even when all other instrumentalists bow and blow their hardest. This puzzled me for a long time, until I discovered that Rossini had an inordinate passion for fresh bologna sandwiches and seemed very particular that they be fresh. So, when he was conducting a performance, he always sent someone out to make sure that the sandwich would be there for him, fresh, at intermission time. In view of the scoring, it seems logical to assume that it was the second oboe player who was entrusted with this vital mission.

Another puzzling question is why "The Barber of Seville" should be the only one of Rossini's operas to survive the test of time. Several of his other operas have music every whit equal to that of "The Barber." "Cenerentola," "The Turk in Italy," "William Tell," all have magnificent scores.

The unflagging popularity of "The Barber" is most likely due to the fact that it is the only one of Rossini's works which has a first-class libretto. There is real dramatic intensity in this tug of war between extremely clever and resourceful people, and the story provides many opportunities for those volcanic explosions that were the hallmark of Rossini's style. No sooner does the public suspect that he has exhausted all possibilities for building up excitement than his music begins to grow still faster and louder.

Because of these musical eruptions, Rossini's contemporaries used to call him "Signor Crescendo" and "Signor Accelerando." In "The Barber" even the gentle, more subdued lyric sections have a way of erupting in a shower of patter, speed, and excitement. We hear such an effect in the third act, where Figaro and the lovers have convinced Don Basilio with the help of a bribe that he is ill and ought to be home in bed. Their farewells start off calmly enough, but their true feeling is soon revealed,

13

like the pop of a champagne bottle. Rosina and Almaviva give a mild hint that Don Basilio should be on his way, but when he's slow about taking the hint the lovers and Figaro grow impatient, and it's not long before we're off to the races.

Even the tender love duet, in the last scene, manages to develop into an exciting feast of chatter.

Since the opera consists, generally speaking, of separate numbers of limited length, Rossini's problem is relatively simple: He starts out quietly and gradually gets faster and louder. There is, however, one scene which is long and uninterrupted—the finale of the first act—and it is here that Rossini's craft is particularly interestnig to observe. Instead of building one rising curve of excitement, the composer manages to introduce three such developments. The initial episode with the drunken soldier becomes more and more furious and, after Figaro's appearance, leads into a regular fight scene. The intervention of the police

15

brings everything to a standstill and gives Rossini a chance to start a new progression of gradual acceleration which leads to the arrest of the soldier and the apparent triumph of Doctor Bartolo's forces. The Count, however, reveals his true identity to the sergeant, who salutes smartly and stands at attention. Doctor Bartolo can scarcely believe his eyes! He remains motionless, as if thunderstruck, and we witness one of those incredible "frozen statue" ensembles which to Rossini serve as the welcome lull before the final storm. He is now ready for the grand demonstration of his art of *crescendo* and *accelerando*. Doctor Bartolo protests vigorously, and we reach the ultimate section, the *vivace,* in which all participants assure us that their heads feel like anvils in some horrible forge: *"Mi par d'esser colla testa in un' orrida fucina."*

Now Rossini is really at home, and he keeps hammering on these anvils until the entire stage seems to go up in smoke!

〰〰〰〰〰〰〰〰

Gioacchino Rossini (1792-1868), with seventeen operas to his credit at the age of twenty-three, signed a contract with Francesco Sforza-Cesarini, the impresario of the Argentina Theatre in Rome, on December 15, 1815. It was stipulated that there should be an important role in the work for the Spanish tenor, Manuel Garcia, but when Rossini read the suggested libretto he dismissed it as vulgar and chose instead the Beaumarchais play, which he rechristened "Almaviva, or The Useless Precaution."

The libretto was started by Pietro Sterbini on January 16, 1816, and the first act delivered to the theatre on February 5, so that the composer could not have taken more than three weeks for the composition itself. For the overture, Rossini went back to a medley of themes from a previous opera, "Aureliano in Palmira," which he had remodelled for his "Elizabeth, Queen of England." "Aureliano" also furnished him with the first of the melodies in "Una voce poco fà."

The first performance of "The Barber" is dated February 20, 1816 by Rossini's biographer, Francis Toye. It was a monumental fiasco. Friends of Giovanni Paisiello, composer of a previous opera on the same subject in 1782, led a cabal in noisy opposition. Manuel Garcia, the tenor, forgot to tune his guitar for the opening Serenade. Vitarelli, the first Basilio, fell and bruised himself badly at his entrance. The popular mezzo-soprano, Gertrude Georgi-Righetti, was warmly received at her aria in the second scene, but the composer, rising from the seat where he was conducting at the piano to applaud the singers,

17

was roundly hissed. Luigi Zamboni (Figaro), and the other members of the cast, Rossi as Berta and Botticelli as Bartolo, were unable to stem the tide of disapproval.

On May 3, 1819, "The Barber" was introduced to New Yorkers at the Park Theater in an English version by Fawcett and Terry, the music adapted by Sir Henry Rowley Bishop. Ten days later there was a benefit performance for the tenor, Thomas Phillips, who took the role of Almaviva. Rosina was sung by the "merry, romping" Catharine Leesugg (later Mrs. Hackett), while John Barnes took the role of Bartolo and Mr. Spiller was Figaro.

The Metropolitan Opera House first presented "The Barber" on November 23, 1883, barely a month after the theater was opened. "The performance was full of buoyancy and spirit" according to William J. Henderson of the Times, while Marcella Sembrich, as Rosina, "displayed the same fine range and quality of voice and wonderful facility of execution as has been heretofore heard." In the music lesson scene she interpolated an aria from "The Magic Flute." Emily Lablache, mother of the first Metropolitan Marthe, Louise Lablache, sang the role of Berta. Giuseppe Del Puente achieved what was deemed "a high degree of merit" as Figaro; Robert Stagno was applauded for his "electrical high notes" as Almaviva. The remainder of the cast comprised Baldassare Corsini as Bartolo, Giovanni Mirabella (Basilio), Ludovico Contini (Fiorello), and Amadeo Grazzi (Soldier). Auguste Vianesi was on the podium.

LA BOHÈME

ON the second of February, 1896, citizens in the city of Turin, Italy, read the following review by the eminent music critic Carlo Bersezio in the newspaper *La Stampa*: "It hurts me very much to have to say it; but frankly this 'Bohème' is not an artistic success. There is much in the score that is empty and downright infantile. The composer should realize that originality can be obtained perfectly well with the old established means, without recourse to consecutive fifths and a disregard of good harmonic rules. 'Bohème' has not made a profound impression on the listeners, and similarly it will not leave much of a trace in the history of the lyric stage. The composer will do wisely if he writes it off as a momentary mistake. Let him just consider 'Bohème' an accidental error in his artistic career." That was the review of the world première of "La Bohème."

Without expecting the critic to be a soothsayer assisted by a never-failing crystal ball, one still wonders why he is often so concerned with petty details that he loses sight of the whole, doesn't see the forest for the trees. One of the most vulnerable attacks the critic can make, it seems to me, is to belabor the composer for breaking the so-called rules of musical composition. History shows us that each great composer in the procession of the centuries has in his turn broken a few more honored precedents and precepts of the past.

The reviewer whom we have quoted objected to Puccini's disregard of good harmonic rules. My objection is not so much with his fault-finding as with the fact that he was so intent on finding so-called errors that he failed to see all the positive virtues of the work, the brilliant theatrical musical ideas which are almost universally admired today. Those consecutive fifths that seemed to have upset Mr. Bersezio, for example, effectively evoke the picture of the gay Christmas celebration in the Latin Quarter of Paris.

Of course, it may be questioned whether that first performance did complete justice to the score, even under the baton of so great a conductor as Arturo Toscanini. The cast did not include any of the best-known singing actors of the time, even in the leading roles. It is also true that only experience and repeated performances of their parts can bring the singers to the point of maximum effectiveness. We normally take that into account when a singer performs a new role, and we use a more lenient standard of judgment than when dealing with a veteran who has sung the part for years.

"Bohème" is largely an ensemble opera, and experience shows that such works require long periods of "shaking down" to achieve adequate performance. Finally, we must not forget that at the first, when one is not thoroughly familiar with a stage work, it is next to impossible to decide whether the lack of ultimate effect lies in the weaknesses of the performance or in the work itself.

The third-act quartet, for example, requires a kind of teamwork and balance among the voices that come only with repeated performances. You can't have that kind of ease at a première.

At the beginning of the act it is Mimi and Rodolfo who are planning on a separation, while Marcello boasts of his happiness with Musetta. However, in the final quartet in this act the situation has reversed itself completely: it is Musetta and Marcello who quarrel and separate, while Mimi and Rodolfo have settled their differences, their lovers' quarrel has vanished, and they are happy once more.

The jealousy and ill-tempered bickering of the one pair and the romantic ardor of the other are subtly woven together throughout this enchanting ensemble. This scene, a masterpiece of operatic composition, demands ensemble work of the highest order on the part of all the participants.

There was also much criticism of "La Bohème" on the ground that it lacked the "big line," that it was constructed out of tiny details and insignificant bits of musical and dramatic material. The realistic trend of operatic composition had its detractors for a long time. Nowadays opera lovers have completely accepted the fact that the world of opera is by no means exclusively inhabited by kings and nobles, gods and heroes, or filled with supercharged passions and world-shattering events. "La Bohème," of course, is a particularly telling example of the down-to-earth trend in operatic composition commonly known as "verismo," (realism). As such, it deals with the simple, ordinary people of this world and the countless little humdrum details of everyday life. Quite apart from any virtue it may have for its own sake, such dramatic realism serves to spark Puccini's musical inventiveness to utterly delightful ends. One comes away from "La Bohème" with the memory not only of big moments of lyrical emotion, for which Puccini is now so justly famous, but also of a thousand little musical touches illustrating the minute details of daily life.

Puccini makes himself a sort of musical master of stage properties. Just as the property man must remember to provide a sheaf of manuscript paper for Rodolfo to tear up in the first act, so Puccini tears up that paper in the music too.

Puccini is also the stage electrician. When Rodolfo and Marcello put the paper in the fire, the fire blazes up in the music for a pitiably brief warming moment.

Then the fire subsides for want of further fuel, despite the encouragement of Rodolfo and his friends. In fact, the fire is so nearly out that Puccini directs the harp to play a seven-fold *pianissimo*.

Puccini is also responsible for sound effects. When Colline tumbles down the stairs in the dark hallway, he takes it philosophically, as a philosopher should, but Puccini's music gives him quite a tumble.

22

A thoroughly charming musical illustration appears in the second act. The horn which Schaunard buys from the junk man is dreadfully out of tune. "What a terrible *RE*," he sings, trying out the horn.

The shabby old coat which Colline is having mended in the second act is as dear to Puccini as to its owner. The composer recognizes something almost like nobility in that coat, shabby though it is, when, in the last act, it is to be sold in the desperate hope of paying for a doctor for the dying Mimi. "Farewell, old friend," Colline sings.

Mimi's little bonnet is another musical prop that reappears with increased poignancy as the action of the opera progresses. In the second act, clinging happily to Rodolfo's arm, she sees the bonnet in a shop, and she must have it.

In the third act, in her farewell to Rodolfo, Mimi sings "Dear one, under my pillow you'll find my little bonnet."

24

In the last act, too, even at the point of death, poor little Mimi can still be gay when Rodolfo shows her the bonnet that he kept to remember their happy days together.

Puccini's musical concern with all these little realistic details adds up to more than cuteness or comedy. It is one of the important means for building his ultimate dramatic effects. All this must have been rather bewildering to many listeners at the turn of the century, listeners who were accustomed to much more grandiose means and seemingly more telling effects.

If the composer of "La Bohème" had his share of critical disfavor, he has also had triumphs far outweighing his disappointments. The millions of listeners at their radios the length and breadth of the land render a verdict too. If I were Puccini, I don't think I should worry too much about what that verdict will be.

Giacomo Puccini (1858-1924) was not at first impressed by the idea of writing an opera based on the "Scènes de la Vie de Bohème" by Henri Murger (1822-1861) when a libretto was offered him by his friend, Ruggiero Leoncavallo, but later accepted another version prepared by his own librettists, Luigi Illica (1857-1919) and Giuseppe Giacosa (1847-1906). The French novelist derived his subject from incidents in the lives of himself (Rodolfo) and his friends Alexandre Schanne (Schaunard), Champfleury (Marcello), Wallon (Colline), Marie-Christine Roux, a model of Ingres (Musetta) and four Parisian midinettes, Lucille, Louisette, Juliette, and Anais (Mimi). Many of the episodes also reflected the composer's own Bohemian days in Milan when he and his friends were given credit by the kindly proprietor of the Café Aïda.

Puccini renounced the libretto in favor of Leoncavallo on July 13, 1894, although the first act had been edited to his satisfaction the previous December and he had composed much of the music. In August, Illica read Puccini the entire libretto, again exciting the composer's interest in the subject. In less than six months the music of the first and second acts was completed, but it was not until November 15, 1895 that the entire score was finished and Puccini summoned his friends to celebrate the event in fancy-dress.

The première at the Royal Opera House in Turin, on February 1, 1896,—just a year before Leoncavallo's opera—was an enthusiastic success with the public. The press, however, was qualified in its approval. The conductor, twenty-nine-year-old Arturo Toscanini, was warmly approved by the composer, who said of him, "When that fellow gets a score into his hands, he digs into it like a miner, in order to explore its every corner and discover its lodes."

The cast was led by Cesira Ferrani, Puccini's first Manon Lescaut, and the twenty-one-year-old tenor Evan Gorga, who, said Puccini, "hasn't got such a bad voice, but I doubt if he will last." The baritone Tieste Wilmant, said Puccini, "is full of good will but a terrible ham." Antonio Pini-Corsi, commended by Puccini's friend the publisher Giulio Ricordi for his good voice but deemed "a singer like a dozen others, and a trivial second-rate actor" was the Schaunard. Camilla Pasini was found, after some search, for the role of Musetta. Palomini was Benoit; Zucchi, Parpignol; Mazzara, Colline.

Immediately after the Turin première, an Italian Company set out for South America under the management of Alfonso Del Conte with the new opera in its repertory. This group was engaged by L. E. Behymer of Los Angeles, who introduced "La Bohème" to the United States on October 14, 1897. The cast comprised Linda Montanari as Mimi; Giuseppe Agostini, a tenor who settled and taught for years in Philadelphia as Rodolfo; Luigi Francesconi, Schaunard; Antonio Fumagalli, Alcindoro and Benoit; Caesar Cioni, Marcello; Vittorio Girardi, Colline; and Cleopatra Vicini, Musetta. The conductor was Pietro Vallini; the Parpignol, Aristide Masiero, three years later sang the same role at the Metropolitan Opera House première.

On this occasion, the day after Christmas, 1900, Nellie Melba's "cold, silvery voice" was noted by the Times. Albert Saléza, the tenor from Bayonne, "was disposed to make too much of the part of Rodolfo," according to the Sun; Giuseppe Campanari was dubbed "a vital figure" by the same critic, and was in "superb voice." Charles Gilibert sang Schaunard; Eugene Dufriche "was comical" as Benoit and Alcindoro; Marcel Journet brought distinction to Colline and Mme. Occhiolini "sang her valse with skill." Luigi Mancinelli conducted.

BORIS GODUNOV

ONCE in a while, some super-sophisticated music lover will make the statement that operatic texts are not supposed to make sense, and that no one in the world really knows what happens in "The Marriage of Figaro" or in "Trovatore." This flippant attitude is understandable. Even if one is familiar with the language, a sung text, unless it is very clearly enunciated, is difficult to follow. Composers, furthermore, do not always feel impelled to present all the information given in a play or a novel and often prefer to limit themselves to a certain number of situations which must suffice for the portrayal of the entire continuity. The reasons for such condensations are both practical and esthetic. To begin with, it takes longer to sing than to speak; therefore there is less time available for the composer to present the necessary information. What is even more to the point, many a sequence which is quite acceptable when read or when presented on the spoken stage is not suitable for musical purposes. What the composer normally does is to select those incidents which he considers fitting for operatic treatment. In the process, important details of the story may go overboard. Most operas, in fact, present only fragments of a story. Tchaikovsky called one of his most famous works, "Lyrical Scenes from Eugene Onegin," and composers could profitably follow his example and thus avoid undeserved criticism. What else is "Trovatore," "Manon," or "Bohème," than "scenes from" these stories.

A listener who is familiar with Abbé Prévost's "Manon Lescaut" or with Murger's "Scènes de la Vie de Bohème" will have no difficulty understanding the operas. Since Gutierrez' play is completely forgotten today, it is no wonder that audiences cannot easily figure out how the eight scenes from "Trovatore" fit together. One can sympathize with the average American spectator witnessing Mussorgsky's "Boris Godunov." The first two scenes take place on the 20th of February and the 1st of March in the year 1598. Five years elapse before the scene in the monastery; the events of the second act, in the Kremlin, occur several months later; the third and fourth acts play in the years 1604 and 1605 respectively. In each act and practically in each scene the listener encounters characters he has not met previously. The leading lady appears only in the third act. Several important characters are introduced in the last act. No wonder that the whole thing gives the impression of being somewhat vague and rambling and without the normal beginning-middle-and-end we have come to expect in the theater.

Things were quite different in Russia on the 27th of January, 1874, when the citizens of St. Petersburg witnessed the première of "Boris Godunov." They had no difficulty at all following the story. All the leading characters were important figures of Russian history, and the spectators knew exactly what to expect. Imagine an American composer writing an opera on the period of the American Revolution. He could pick out those aspects of the life and times of Washington and his associates which he found most interesting for musical purposes and not bother to explain every situation in detail. The Russians, in a way, had the benefit of a double indoctrination; not only were they acquainted with the historical background of the story, but they were even more intimately familiar with Pushkin's drama upon which the libretto was modeled. Pushkin's work consists of twenty-three episodes from which Mussorgsky chose his ten scenes—in most instances preserving Pushkin's text, much of which every educated Russian knows by heart.

29

There are in the opera two separate series of events, one dealing with the guilty Tsar, the other with the false Dimitri. Half the incidents are centered around Boris, the other half deal with the career of the pretender. The Tsar and Dimitri never come face to face, which explains the variety of characters and the seemingly disconnected nature of the episodes.

We should accept the fact that many operatic texts give us only partial information. The composer takes it for granted that we are acquainted with the details of the plot, and, as good listeners, we might as well coöperate with him and learn the background of the story beforehand. It is only then that we will appreciate the more subtle aspects of both the composition and the performance.

To return to the premiére of "Boris Godunov," we need not envy those present on that occasion. While it is true that the story was no stumbling block, Mussorgsky's music confused them all the more. In that respect, today's audiences are much better prepared. The shapes of Mussorgsky's melodies and his occasional harmonic harshnesses do not frighten us. We look forward to many a familiar and justly celebrated section, such as the Coronation scene, Boris' famous monologues in the second and last acts, the Polonaise and the love-duet of the third act, and the haunting lament of the Simpleton. The more carefully we listen, the more charming finesses will be revealed to us. Mussorgsky had exceptionally sharp and perceptive ears and an extraordinary gift for transforming all sorts of sounds into vivid musical equivalents. Of course, "tone-painting" is an old story in music. In opera particularly, where the words, the action, and the scenic picture help to direct the attention and to stimulate the association of ideas, composers have always liked to mimic all sorts of man-made as well as natural sounds. We remember the operatic storms and battle-scenes, twittering birds, hunting horns, and shepherds' pipes.

The remarkable thing about Mussorgsky is that he expands this art of musical imitation to include not only the more obvious sounds but almost any sort of noise heard by human ears.

In the scene at the inn, for example, there is a complete musical picture of a man taking a drink. The wine is poured . . . he smacks his lips . . . drinks . . . pauses to taste the flavor . . . it is good . . . he smacks his lips again . . . drinks it up . . . more wine is poured, and this helping is again emptied in two gulps:

At the end of this scene, the breaking of the window is quite clearly shown:

In the palace scene there is another unusual musical illustration. There is a clock with a set of revolving mechanical figures.

31

We hear the ticking of the clock and the whirring of the un-winding spring:

Mussorgsky was particularly devoted to the musical portrayal of church bells. In the opening of the Forest Scene, we hear the tocsin sounding the alarm:

The pealing of the Coronation bells is treated by the composer with loving attention. One of the Kremlin's little bells has a slight imperfection, and Mussorgsky delights in reproducing even this detail in the music.

Mussorgsky, however, is not content to let music imitate merely sounds. Apparently almost everything he *saw*, as well as what he heard, suggested music to him. Motions and gestures became converted into music. In the scene in the monastery, the old monk, Pimen, sits working at his desk. Maybe something could have been done musically with the scratching of the pen, but Mussorgsky hit on an even more characteristic feature of the act of writing, the motion involved. As one writes, the hand moves constantly in a steady up and down movement within a very narrow compass. And that is exactly how Mussorgsky describes musically the act of writing:

ANDANTE TRANQUILLO

When Pimen pauses in his writing, it stops. When he resumes, it starts again.

Even the simplest means of musical illustration can be effective, if they are done with subtlety. One of the most primitive devices consists in having the music move toward the treble to illustrate some *upward* movement and, conversely, *down*, into the bass for the opposite direction. Mussorgsky takes advantage of this device in the first act, in the sequence dealing with Grigori's dream. The novice relates to Pimen how he dreamed of *climbing* a great tower and then looking *down* at Moscow lying at his feet, while the crowd below jeered and hooted at him. All this is faithfully reproduced in the music: the steep ladder that leads up the tower:

the people below that seem like ants in an anthill:

the laughter of the crowd:

Maybe the most startling of these translations into music occurs in the second act when the mistress of the inn explains to Grigori that although the direct road to Lithuania has been closed, there is a detour, a round-about way which he can follow to get there. Mussorgsky identifies Lithuania by the key of C major, and shows two progressions by which it can be reached. The direct route is illustrated by a simple move in the harmony; in fact about the simplest possible way to establish a tonality:

35

The detour is brilliantly indicated by a harmonic progression that, at first, seems to move far away from the goal of C major:

"Turn left," he is told, "then take the pathway to the chapel at Chekan . . . thence proceed to Khlopino, and to Zaitsevo . . . " the music has followed every move and reached Zaitsevo:

"From here", says the innkeeper, "any little boy can show you the way to Lithuania," and the composer via a simple and naive modulation, lands us safely and surely in C major.

The whole idea of the two roads seems at first completely unrelated to music, and yet Mussorgsky, in his uncanny way, finds a perfect illustration for it.

The upraised hand wielding the whip was for Mussorgsky symbolic of police brutality and oppression. And the instruments in the orchestra faithfully depict this threatening gesture in music:

As a matter of fact, the policemen of the prologue and those of the tavern scene are illustrated by the same musical figure, although they are different individuals. The phrase becomes for the composer the musical mark of the profession. By superimposing this phrase upon the lovely folk song melody in the orchestral introduction to the work, Mussorgsky symbolically points up the plight of the oppressed Russian people, which is the central theme of the opera.

After all, it is the simple common people of Russia about whom this opera was written, and to portray this suffering, inarticulate "soul of Russia" Mussorgsky chose the Simpleton, the harmless, innocent, halfwit, a figure regarded with religious awe in olden times. He sings a strange and very moving prophetic lament:

37

This lament for the people of Russia might be called the very heart of Mussorgsky's masterwork.

Much has been written recently regarding the relative merits of Mussorgsky's original version as compared with the Rimsky-Korsakov edition. Now that the original version has become part of the regular repertory of the Metropolitan Opera Company, repeated hearings will permit an objective evaluation of both versions. The examples included in this "accent" have been quoted from the original musical text.

The composer, Modeste Mussorgsky (1839-1881), based his plot on the drama of Alexander Pushkin (1799-1837) and the history of Russia by Nikolai Karamzin (1766-1826). The music was written between October, 1868, and May, 1869, while the score was completed by the following December (Version I). After rejection by the directorate of the Imperial Theatres of St. Petersburg in 1870, the composer made extensive alterations between April, 1871, and July, 1872, adding Boris' Kremlin monologue, the Forest of Kromy, and the two Polish scenes (Version II). Three scenes from this version were performed at the Maryinski Theatre on February 3, 1873.

In the middle of January, 1874, a week before the world première, appeared Version III, the first published edition, in which the first act was referred to as a prologue. After the death of the composer, his friend, Rimsky-Korsakov (1844-1908), brought forth Version IV, deleting many scenes, polishing the orchestration, making alterations in both the vocal line and the harmony, adding key signatures, and placing the Kromy scene before the death of Boris. Just before his death, Rimsky-Korsakov made a second revision (Version V) reinstating many of his earlier cuts. Later editions have attempted to realize Mussorgsky's original intentions, compensating meanwhile for his alleged technical limitations.

In 1926 the British house of Chester published Version VI. In 1928-29 the Oxford University Press issued Dr. Paul Lamm's full orchestral edition (Version VII). Dimitri Shostakovich undertook further revision during World War II (Version VIII), and in 1952 Karol Rathaus combined Version III with the orchestral sketches from which Version VII was made. The resultant score was first heard in a new English adaptation by John Gutman, on March 6, 1953, at the Metropolitan Opera House.

The première of "Boris Godunov" took place on January 24, 1874, at the Imperial Opera House in St. Petersburg as a benefit for Julia Feodorovna Platonova, who insisted that this work be chosen for the purpose and herself sang the role of Marina. Alexander Melnikov sang the title role. Another early enthusiast for the work was Komissarjevsky, who sang Dimitri. Sobolev impersonated both Shchelkalov and Missail as well as the Boyar

39

and Tcherniakovsky. Vassiliev's name appears beside the roles of Shuisky, Pimen, and Lavitzki. Krutikov and Raab were Boris' son and daughter. Kondraviev sang Rangoni; Petrov was Varlaam; Abarinova the Innkeeper; Bulakhov the Simpleton; Liadov both the Police Official and Mityukh. Matveev sang Krustchov. Eduard Napravnik conducted.

Arturo Toscanini introduced "Boris" to the United States in the familiar Rimsky-Korsakov version on March 19, 1913. The language chosen was Italian, the settings being imported from Paris, where they had been originally designed by A. Golovine and Benois.

Adamo Didur's impersonation of the Tsar entitled him to "a new position in the public estimation," wrote William J. Henderson in the Sun, while Paul Althouse, making his debut as Dimitri, was reckoned "a valuable acquisition." Louise Homer sang Marina; Anna Case and Leonora Sparkes acted the royal son and daughter. Maria Duchène was the Nurse and Jeanne Maubourg the Innkeeper. Angelo Bada sang Shuisky; Leon Rothier was Pimen; Andreas de Segurola "gave a remarkably thrilling and vivid impersonation of Varlaam," according to the Times. Vincenzo Reschiglian sang both Shchelkalov and Lavitsky. Pietro Audisio was Missail; Giulio Rossi, the Official; Albert Reiss, the Simpleton and Louis Kreidler, Tcherniakovsky.

CARMEN

MANY people are not aware that the form in which "Carmen" is presented today is different from the way it was originally composed and performed. The orchestrally accompanied and sung recitatives which are now usually heard wherever "Carmen" is produced were added by Bizet's intimate friend, Ernest Guiraud, shortly after Bizet's death in the summer of 1875. They were intended for those opera houses which objected to the use of spoken dialogue. It is with these Giraud recitatives that "Carmen" is published and known throughout the world.

Besides this major change, the published version of the opera shows several other departures from the composer's original intentions. There are, in fact, at least six portions of varying length and importance which have been omitted in the printed score. The attempt to restore these sections has led to a worldwide search, and some of the missing sections are yet to be located. The original detective work was relatively simple. The basic text of the opera by Meilhac and Halévy is available, and one finds in it several episodes which are new to the "Carmen" lover. There is, for instance, a solo for Morales following the opening chorus and scene with Micaela. Morales describes to the other soldiers a scene which unfolds on the square and chuckles as he relates how a young cavalier manages to pass a love note to a young wife in the presence of her old husband. The music of this episode, as it happens, is quite charming and in every way worthy of Bizet's "Carmen;" yet it is easy to under-

41

stand why the scene was omitted. The story it tells is completely extraneous to the plot of the opera and delays the introduction of the main characters and the exposition of the drama.

Less forgivable is the other omission from the first act. As we know the opera, we hear, soon after the factory bell has rung, a choral section for the tenors. The gay cavaliers of Seville await the pretty workers returning from lunch to the cigarette factory and boast of the romantic and amorous remarks they will make to the girls. When the cigarette makers do come back, the tenors apparently become tongue-tied, and yet, as the young ladies smoke their cigarettes, they mention that these words of love are just about as important as the smoke which rises from their cigarettes. In the original version the cavaliers were less reticent, but as the opera is known today their amorous declarations have all been deleted.

The second act shows only a minor deviation from the original —Carmen mimicking Don José's appeal, *"C'est mal à toi, Carmen"* (how cruel of you, Carmen) during the duet. The irony and sarcasm with which she pretends not to believe José's words of love are enormously effective, and one cannot see any reason why this short and potent episode had to be omitted.

The most important cut has been executed on the fight scene between José and Escamillo in the third act. From contemporary reports we gather that the first few performances included the complete fight scene, in which Escamillo wins the first encounter but generously refuses to take advantage of his victim. It must have been at some later moment that it was decided to shorten this scene—perhaps because it calls for considerable athletic prowess, which put too much of a strain on the rather portly tenors and baritones of the time. And yet the inclusion of this section offers a definite advantage, both dramatically and musically. The character of Escamillo, otherwise treated sketchily, is greatly enhanced and enriched by the addition of this section. It also explains a sentence in the published score which otherwise makes no sense. After Carmen manages to rescue Escamillo from being killed by her enraged lover, the bullfighter addresses Don José in these words: "As for you, handsome soldier, we are even now, and I am ready for a playoff at any time."

The most obvious source for the music of these missing sections is Bizet's original manuscript-score, but the recent examination of a microfilm showed that three of these sections (all but Carmen's sarcastic repetition of Don José's plea in the second act) had been removed from the score. Although the page numbering was changed to compensate for these excisions, the original pagination is still visible on the margin and permits one to estimate the exact number of pages removed.

From this point on the search for the missing sections assumes the character of a hunt for hidden treasure. The excised pages of the manuscript-score have not yet been found, but in the British Museum a rare copy of an early printing of the piano-vocal score, demonstrates Morales' solo in the first act and the entire fight scene in the third act, reproduced in full. The music of the amorous cavaliers has yet to be unearthed!

While the manuscript score is disappointing in this regard, it unexpectedly rewards us with the presence of some music the existence of which we didn't even suspect. One is a delightful march for the change of guard. It takes place between the two children's choruses of the first act and consists of a contrapuntal conversation between a solo violin and a solo 'cello to a *pizzicato* accompaniment by the rest of the strings. The other is a fourteen-measure bridge passage between the B minor ending of the Seguidilla and the F minor beginning of the Finale of the first act.

By now most of the missing portions of the score which could be reconstructed have been performed here and there, and it is to be hoped that in time most opera lovers will have a chance to become acquainted with Bizet's original "Carmen."

In comparing the original dialogues with Guiraud's recitatives, one finds that both versions have much to recommend them. Since it takes considerably longer to sing a line than to speak it, Guiraud had to make extensive cuts in the original spoken dialogue, and many dramatic subtleties went overboard in the process.

In the present version of "Carmen," for instance, the two smugglers, Dancaire and Remendado, are practically twins—conventional comic opera bandits. In the original spoken version, however, their dialogue differentiates them neatly. Dancaire is definitely the boss of the band, while Remendado is a happy-go-lucky fellow with a certain elegance of manner and a delightful sense of humor.

When Don José meets Carmen at the inn in the second act, another lapse is noticeable. The dialogue has been so drastically cut that we are hardly aware the soldier has been in jail for two months on her account. The whole episode is dismissed as if he had merely stepped out to get the evening paper.

Musically speaking, however, Guiraud did a splendid piece of work. He captured the style of Bizet to perfection and drew on the original themes to characterize the situations and personalities with which he was concerned. When Don José picks up the flower thrown him by Carmen in the first act, for instance, he is left alone with his thoughts:

"What a look she gave me," he muses, "what effrontery!" As he sings, the music recalls Carmen's entrance:

"This flower might have been a bullet aimed straight at my heart," he continues. The orchestra meanwhile suggests that José has indeed met his fate.

"The perfume is strong and the flower is beautiful. And the woman? If there are such things as sorceresses, she certainly is one of them." Guiraud invokes Carmen's seductive "Habanera" from the orchestra.

The world-wide acceptance of the published version incorporating Guiraud's recitatives has probably established the work in this form for all time. There is no reason, however, why performances of Bizet's original, with the spoken dialogues and the inclusion of at least some of the now recovered sections, should not prove an attractive and valuable addition to our operatic life.

45

The composer Georges Bizet (1838-1875), following the success of his incidental music to "L'Arlésienne" (1872), was approached by Camille du Locle, director of the Paris Opéra-Comique, to write an opera to a libretto by a cousin of Mme. Bizet, Ludovic Halévy (1834-1908) and Henri Meilhac (1831-1897). This text was founded on a story by Prosper Mérimée (1803-1870), inspired by the researches of George Henry Borrow (1803-1881), in the life of the gypsies of Spain.

The composer conceived the entire score in his mind before putting pen to paper and wrote the twelve hundred pages of the orchestration in two months. He frequently rewrote a troublesome passage, however, and he made thirteen versions of the "Habanera," based on Yradier's song "El Areglito." Micaela's third act aria was borrowed from Bizet's score for "Grisélidis."

"Carmen" was first produced at the Opéra-Comique on March 3, 1875, with spoken dialogues which were replaced by musical recitatives for a later Vienna performance. These were written by Ernest Guiraud (1837-1892) after Bizet's death on June 3, 1875, only three months after the première. It is said that the composer's death from a heart attack or an embolism, at the age of thirty-seven, was hastened by his disappointment at the severity of the critics and the shocked attitude of the public toward his masterpiece, but this is contradicted by the success which "Carmen" enjoyed at its second and subsequent performances.

The first Carmen was Célestine Galli-Marié, who is said to have considered her role immoral, and who was nevertheless accused of playing up its coarseness. The first Don José, Paul

Lhérie, was actually a baritone who achieved some success by singing the final measures of the "Flower Song" in falsetto, but he never attempted another tenor role. Jacques Bouhy, the first Escamillo, had an exceptionally extended range which permitted him to cope with both Rigoletto and Méphistophélès. Mmes. Chapuy, Ducasse, and Chevalier were responsible for the interpretations of Micaela, Frasquita, and Mercédès, while the Messrs. Potel, and Barnoit were Dancaire and Remendado. Messrs. Dufriche, Duvernoy, and Nathan impersonated Zuniga, Morales, and Lillas Pastia. The conductor was M. Deloffre.

The eventual popularity of "Carmen" was increased by Minnie Hauk, a New York soprano who introduced the role to New Yorkers, rising from a sick bed to sing it in Italian at the Academy of Music on October 23, 1878. She later took it all over the world, singing it over six hundred times. Her Don José was Italo Campanini and her Escamillo, Giuseppe del Puente, both of whom were later chosen to portray the roles at the Metropolitan. Both men earned the approval of the Sun critic, the former for "the perfect ease and roundness" of his voice, the latter for his brilliant characterization. Messrs. Franceschi and Bolli took the roles of Zuniga and Morales; Mmes. Sinico, Robiati, and Lablache those of Micaela, Frasquita, and Mercédès, while Messrs. Grazzi and Thierry impersonated Dancaire and Remendado.

"Carmen" was introduced to the Metropolitan Opera public during the inaugural season on January 9, 1884, under the baton of Cleofonte Campanini. Zelia Trebelli (born Zelia Gilbert) sang the title role in Italian, trying to make her Carmen "a beautiful demon," according to Mr. Krehbiel in the Tribune, but lacking "lightness and grace in the earlier moments." The Micaela, Alwina Valleria, was the first American to sing at the Metropolitan, and proved "the vocal success of the opera." Italo

Campanini "was in bad voice but acted with telling fervor . . . the most powerful piece of acting that has been seen on the stage this season." Giuseppe Del Puente reappeared as Escamillo.

Ida Corani and Louise Lablache were the gypsies. Achille Augier was the Zuniga, Ludovico Contini the Morales, while Baldassare Corsini sang Dancaire and Amadeo Grazzi, Remendado, all of them criticized by Mr. Krehbiel for "poor singing and acting" which was not improved by "wretched stage management."

CAVALLERIA RUSTICANA

IMAGINE being a member of a quiz panel and having to answer a question concerning the identity of a certain opera: give the name of a popular Italian lyric drama, the action of which takes place on an important church holiday in the second half of the nineteenth century and deals with villagers living in the southern part of Italy. The work is divided into two sections separated by an orchestral interlude. The plot is roughly this: a devoted husband is totally unaware that his wife deceives him with a lover. So we have a wife, a husband, and a lover: the eternal triangle. But the triangle is squared, so to speak, by a very important addition musically and dramatically. There is a fourth person who, having excellent reasons to hate the unfaithful wife, decides to take vengeance on her by revealing the truth to her husband. The husband's outraged feelings are stunningly portrayed as the first part of the work comes to a close. The second part of the opera begins quite gaily, but soon the husband appears, and things begin to happen. In fact, to make a long story short, before the final curtain falls the lover has been killed by the husband.

By this time, the reader undoubtedly has realized that this is a trick question, and that, in spite of all the detail given, everything mentioned applies equally well to two operas: Mascagni's "Cavalleria Rusticana" and Leoncavallo's "Pagliacci."

The church holiday is Easter in "Cavalleria" and the Feast of the Assumption in "Pagliacci"; the settings are Sicily and Calabria, respectively. Keeping the traditional order by having

"Cavalleria" precede "Pagliacci," we may say that the husbands, Alfio and Canio, are deceived by their wives, Lola and Nedda, the lovers being Turiddu and Silvio. And in each case the husband kills the lover. The informer in both operas is motivated by jealousy; in "Cavalleria" it is a woman, Santuzza, who is in love with Turiddu; in "Pagliacci," it is a man, Tonio, the crippled clown, who has been repulsed by Nedda.

It is very possible that the reader has never before realized to what extent the plots of the two operas run in parallel grooves. The spectator in the opera house is certainly totally unaware of these resemblances, mainly because the musical and dramatic treatment given these plots is so different. Musically speaking, the differences are certainly more important than the resemblances.

In "Pagliacci," the significant characteristic lies in the contrast between the music allotted to the make-believe comedy of masks and that given to the real life situations. The chapter devoted to "Pagliacci" will deal with this theme in some detail.

"Cavalleria Rusticana," although lacking the extra dimension of the play-within-a-play, is by no means devoid of its own subtleties. It is the most vigorous representative of *verismo*, the "truth" school, which served as a shot in the arm for Italian opera at the moment when the operatic world had grown weary of carefully mannered sentiment and grandiloquent romance. According to Webster's dictionary, *verismo* is defined as "the theory that in art and literature the ugly and the vulgar have their place on the grounds of truth and esthetic value."

Giovanni Verga, the Italian novelist, wrote a short story called "Cavalleria Rusticana" that was said to be founded in fact and then made a play from it. This was the material drawn on by G. Targioni-Tozzetti and G. Menasci when Mascagni asked them for a libretto. Thus the opera is true to life, or at least to the melodramatic kind of life we read about in sensational newspapers.

Mascagni was only twenty-six when he learned that a contest for one-act operas was being sponsored by the publisher Edoardo Sonzogno. Always in need, wandering about from one small post to another, Mascagni dashed off the work in a fury of inspiration and staked everything on this one gamble.

There were no less than seventy-three operas submitted. The judges were not aware of the identity of the composers. Each work received a number, and the author was known only by a motto. Mascagni's number was thirty-one and his motto PAX. When he sent in his manuscript, Mascagni did not include the orchestral introduction. It was, as he said, "too risky." He felt that the tenor's serenade breaking in on the prelude from behind the curtain represented such a radical break with operatic tradition, that it might prejudice the judges against his work. It was only at the time of the final examination, when he was asked to play and sing the opera for the jury, that Mascagni decided to bring the Prelude with him, and the judges granted him permission to append it to his work even at that late date. Great was the joy of the young composer when the winners were announced and he saw his work crowned along with that of two others: Vincenzo Ferroni's "Rudello" and Niccola Spinelli's "Labilla." On the night of the première, May 17th, 1890, the audience at the Costanzi Theater, in Rome, was skeptical; no one had ever heard of this young Mascagni. When the conductor, Mugnone, started the Prelude, the listeners were inattentive, but at the first tones of the tenor's Siciliana from behind the curtain the audience became fully aroused.

The roar of applause and *"bravos"* at the end of the Prelude was deafening—according to reports of eye-witnesses not a single spectator remained seated. This set the tone for the rest of the evening, and the première was the first of "Cavalleria's" innumerable triumphs all over the world.

As far as the *verismo* movement is concerned, it is well to remember that composers of all periods aimed at believable portrayal and exactness of characterization. Whether they called it *"la nature,"* which Gluck favored, or precision of dramatic utterance, as Verdi's devotion to the *"parola scenica"* indicates, they all wanted to create real people and sincerity of expression.

What is convincing and believable depends on one's background and knowledge as much as on general ideas prevailing in different epochs and among different peoples. In that respect even Verga and Mascagni showed certain basic disagreement. There exists a very interesting letter written by the playwright to a German producer of the spoken "Cavalleria." Verga recommends to the actors a restrained type of behavior and points out that Sicilians are not apt to show emotion. In Verga's words, the Sicilian peasant is very much like the Oriental, outwardly impassive and calm. Alfio, in particular, should not, according to Verga, display visible emotion when he learns of his wife's infidelity! One needs only to think of the explosive music of the duet between Santuzza and Alfio to see how impossible such an attitude would be in Mascagni's opera. Musically speaking, *verismo* means violence of expression. In "Cavalleria," that quality of raw passion, of emotion almost vulgarly displayed, is set to music that matches these moods perfectly. This is the reason the work continues to hold a fascinated public in its spell year after year.

In spite of this straightforwardness of approach, Mascagni's "Cavalleria" is by no means devoid of subtleties. One of the most interesting occurs in the song in which Alfio praises the joys of his profession and then proceeds to sing the praises of his faithful wife, Lola. The orchestral accompaniment to the first verse is couched in the regular um-pah rhythm wherein the bass notes of the orchestra coincide with the accents of the words:

In the second verse, when Alfio speaks of his wife, the orchestral rhythms are reversed. Instead of the normal um-pah, um-pah, we hear pah-um, pah-um! It is as if the orchestra were trying to show Alfio how mistaken he is in believing his wife to be faithful!

Curiously enough, Mascagni has accidentally hit here upon a device which was developed to its full potential a whole generation later by Igor Stravinsky. Orchestral rhythms that flatly contradict the normal speech accents of the singers are a regular Stravinskian trademark, as we will have occasion to note in discussing his "Rake's Progress." The alternation of úm-pah, and pah-úm patterns is used by Stravinsky with particular success in his opera "Mavra."

It is fascinating to observe how artistic ideas of successive generations interact and mingle. The novelty of yesterday may seem old-fashioned today, but the inspirations of the exceptional mind survive all the fashions and conventions, and the masterworks of each period continue to warm the hearts of audiences everywhere.

Pietro Mascagni (1863-1945) wrote "Cavalleria Rusticana" as an ambitious move to win fame and fortune. The text was based by his librettists, Giovanni Targioni-Tozzetti (1863-1934) and Guido Menasci (1867-1925), on a one-act play by the celebrated Italian novelist, Giovanni Verga (1840-1922), who had adapted it from his story published in 1880. The opera won a prize offered by the Sonzogno music publishers and attained instant popularity.

Its première took place at the Costanzi Theater in Rome under the baton of Leopold Mugnone, on May 17, 1890. Gemma Bellincioni sang the role of Santuzza opposite her former teacher, Roberto Stagno, whom she had married nine years before. Other members of the cast were A. Galli as Lola, Salassi as Alfio, and F. Casali as Lucia.

The immediate fame of "Cavalleria Rusticana" caused a race for the first American production. Gustav Hinrichs, a former assistant to Theodore Thomas who had organized his own company in Philadelphia, conducted the first performance in this country at the Grand Opera House in that city. Nineteen days later Minnie Hauk sang Santuzza for the first time in Chicago, and within the week one Rudolph Aronson offered the New York première in the afternoon of October 1, followed by Oscar Hammerstein's presentation at another theater in the evening.

The first Santuzza in the United States was Selma Kört-Kronold, a Polish soprano who also created Nedda before American audiences. The first Lola both in Philadelphia and Chicago was Helen Dudley-Campbell, singing on both occasions opposite her husband, Giuseppe Del Puente, the first Alfio. Albert Guille was the Turiddu and Jennie Teal, Mamma Lucia.

Within three months of its American première, "Cavalleria Rusticana" reached the Metropolitan stage. On December 30, 1891, at a signal from the baton of Auguste Vianesi, the curtains parted to disclose Lola's house, behind which Fernando

Valero sang Turiddu's Siciliana. "Winning a call in spite of his stridulous voice and singular phrasing," according to Mr. Krehbiel, "the tenor stepped out from cover, bowed his acknowledgments, and, returning to his hiding place, serenaded his love over again." Emma Eames "wore a perfectly exquisite accordion-pleated skirt as the distraught Sicilian peasant" (Santuzza), continues Mr. Krehbiel. Giulia Ravogli, after singing the first Metropolitan Orfeo earlier in the evening, returned to impersonate Lola. Edoardo Camera, who had made his debut as Count di Luna a fortnight before, was the Alfio, and the tireless Mathilde Bauermeister sang Mamma Lucia.

COSÌ FAN TUTTE

"COSÌ FAN TUTTE" is no longer considered silly, frivolous, wicked, or little more than a marionette play. It is much more than an amusing farce, in spite of the elements of a wager, the use of disguises, and a rather cruel joke carried to extremes. The practical joke stems from the wager itself. In the first scene, Don Alfonso challenges the lovers, Ferrando and Guglielmo, with the statement that all women, including their beloved Dorabella and Fiordiligi, are fickle. To prove him wrong, the two men make a bet with him, and to prove his point Alfonso insists that for twenty-four hours the men must follow all of his instructions. In a sense, it is a shabby trick, for the two men to disguise themselves and then come back, each trying to break down the resistance of the other's fiancée.

Some writers of the nineteenth century took the view that Fiordiligi and Dorabella were immoral because they succumbed so quickly. They forgot that Mozart was not dealing with a realistic period of time, but with a device of the theater of his day. We must remember that the theatrical convention of Mozart's century made it mandatory that the action of a play be limited to a twenty-four hour period. If Mozart had lived a generation later, he might easily have made the time limit of the bet longer and thereby avoided the impression that the young ladies were completely unprincipled. The music, at any rate, proves that Mozart found his heroines lovable and entirely human. No wonder! In a sense the situation repeated something of Mozart's own life. At first he was in love with Aloysia Weber,

57

but he later married her younger sister, Constanze, so the dilemma of a romance involving two equally attractive sisters was, for Mozart, much more than a farce.

We see the genius of Mozart in his treatment of this plot and his understanding of the characters in it. We have two pairs of lovers and a pair of philosophers. The philosophers, the cynical Don Alfonso and the clever maid Despina, remain pretty much the same throughout the opera. But the lovers change, and it is this transformation which is one of the subtle and interesting points of the story and the music.

When we first meet the men and, later, the two sisters, we find little to distinguish Ferrando from Guglielmo, or Fiordiligi from Dorabella. In the opening scene, neither man thinks his sweetheart could possibly deceive him, and each asserts his faith with pretty much the same music. Ferrando starts off praising Dorabella:

Then Guglielmo sings of his faith in Fiordiligi:

The girls also are of one mind at first. We discover them in the second scene singing of their devotion to the men. Their duet ends in thirds and sixths, an obvious musical device showing that each one thinks in the same terms about the one she loves. They are in full agreement.

We first find a difference between the men when, after pretending to go off to war, they return disguised as two Albanians. Something seems to happen to them, as though, after assuming these disguises, they show their true colors. They are much less inhibited and react more naturally. Guglielmo, the baritone, emerges as the more aggressive. He is inclined to take the initiative, and makes the first advance to the ladies.

Ferrando is more soft-hearted, romantic, and even idealistic. He is quite rhapsodic about Dorabella's persistent devotion to him.

59

Soon Mozart begins to differentiate between the basic character of the sisters. The younger, Dorabella, emerges as the more adventurous, and Guglielmo is able to press his advantage to the point where she is not only willing to listen but is definitely interested. Fiordiligi, on the other hand, remains for the time being as steadfast as the rock of which she sang in the first act.

When Guglielmo shows Ferrando his own locket, which Dorabella had given to Guglielmo, Ferrando is grief-stricken and disillusioned, and his music is quite melodramatic.

Guglielmo, for his part, cannot refrain from a bit of delicious bragging: After all, what girl could forget him?

And, obviously Fiordiligi is an exception. It takes a great deal to break her down: seven pleas of undying love, several threats of suicide, and two hours of Mozart's most glorious music.

Another trait of individuality emerges when Guglielmo, our proud, boasting man-about-women, is shown that even he can be forgotten. Ferrando was grief-stricken but resigned at Dorabella's infidelity, but when Guglielmo learns that Fiordiligi has accepted the disguised Ferrando's plea, he wants to burst in and tear somebody apart. Even in the wedding scene, we find Guglielmo is still the individualist. Ferrando accepts Alfonso's advice and adapts himself to the new situation. But not Guglielmo. During the ensemble in the wedding scene, the voice of each of the lovers enters in turn singing the music of the "toast".

When it comes to Guglielmo, what do we hear? *"Ah, bevessero del tossico."* He wishes the girls were drinking poison. One would think that, after all the boasting he has done, a little humiliation might be in order.

The music tells us that Mozart found these people human, the men as much at fault as the women. In the end that seems to sum up the whole plot. There is no doubt that Mozart was clearly aware of the humanity of his characters, and it is this conviction, translated into his music, which makes "Così Fan Tutte" contemporary even one hundred and sixty years after it first saw the light of day.

The plot of "Così Fan Tutte" is said to have been based on an actual incident that took place during the carnival season of 1789 in Vienna. The Emperor Joseph II, returning to his capital, depressed, from the Turkish front, was so amused by the story that he asked Lorenzo da Ponte (1749-1838) to turn it into a libretto. Wolfgang Amadeus Mozart (1756-1791), whose "Nozze di Figaro" had just enjoyed a successful revival in Vienna, was commissioned to write the music and presented with the libretto on November 2, 1789. The composer's fortunes were at a low ebb that autumn. Deep in debt, forced to move from his suburban home into a cheaper apartment in the center of the city, saddened by the death of an infant daughter and the illness of his wife, Mozart wrote to his friend, the merchant Michael Puchberg on December 29, asking for an advance of 400 gulden (about $200) and quoting the payment he would soon receive from the new opera (200 ducats, or $450, as security). The opera seems to have been written in great haste, with many abbreviations in the autograph score. Its sprightly gaiety, however, gives no hint of the composer's distress at the time.

The première of "Così Fan Tutte" took place at the Burgtheater on January 26, 1790. The Emperor, indisposed, was absent, and never witnessed the work he had commissioned, dying four weeks later at the age of forty-eight. The two sisters, Fiordiligi and Dorabella, were impersonated by two singers who themselves were sisters. The first, Adriana Gabrielli-Del Bene, known as the Ferrarese, was the mistress of the librettist, who maintained that "she rendered indispensable services" on the stage. Some authorities, however, hint that Mozart wrote at least one aria to show up and make fun of her limitations. Her sister, the Dorabella, was known as Louise Villeneuve. Dorotea and Francesco Bussani, who played Despina and Don Alfonso, were husband and wife, a pair of rascals, according to da Ponte, backstage intriguers whose morals were as weak as their art. History reports, however, that they sang well and projected their comedy with skill and effectiveness. Francesco Benucci was the Guglielmo, hailed by the biographer Jahn for his "round, full, fine bass voice." Ferrando was Vincenzo Calvesi; the conductor, Mozart himself.

"Così Fan Tutte" did not reach the United States until 1922, when it was presented at the Metropolitan Opera House on March 24. On this occasion a large audience was beguiled by what Richard Aldrich of the Times called a "thrice-admirable performance." Florence Easton "conquered the stupendous diffi-

63

culties of the score," according to Mr. Krehbiel of the Tribune, singing with what Mr. Aldrich called "a true perception of Mozart's style." In the role of Dorabella, Frances Peralta "disclosed her abilities as actress and singer" (in Mr. Krehbiel's words), while Giuseppe De Luca as Guglielmo was "delightful in his beautiful singing of the music as in the unctuous humor of his action." Lucrezia Bori "was very pretty, saucy, arch, and mischievous in her representation of Despina" (Aldrich) and "sang the music charmingly." George Meader was praised by the same critic for his "intelligence and appreciation" of the role of Ferrando, while Adamo Didur was hailed as "richly humorous and cynical." Arthur Bodanzky's conducting, concluded the Times review, "brought to pass a performance finished, spirited, brilliant, one that may be said to have given a true account of Mozart's work."

DON CARLO

AMONG the operas of Giuseppe Verdi, "Don Carlo" ranks as one of the most ambitious. In its dimensions, colors, and contrasts, it resembles a huge painting executed in bold strokes and many hues, bright and dark. Its characters are not only caught in their own personal emotions and passions, they are also actors in a dark drama of dangerous political intrigue.

It was not easy for Verdi to tell the story, or rather the many stories, of this opera within the limitations of what could be considered an opera of reasonable length, and his textwriters did a remarkable piece of work in condensing Schiller's play into a libretto. Even so, the operatic plot is not easy to follow, since it covers several dramatic aspects at the same time. Politics, religion and human relations are all part of the story.

To begin with, we have two unusual love-triangles in the opera. King Philip and his son, Don Carlo, are both in love with Queen Elisabeth, Philip's third wife and Carlo's stepmother.

The ladies face a similar predicament. Queen Elisabeth and the Princess Eboli are both in love with Don Carlo.

The love between the Queen and the young Prince, between stepmother and stepson, is, of course, utterly hopeless. Through his music Verdi conveys this feeling of hopelessness, of a love that can never materialize. Such music is of a very unusual nature for Verdi, a heart-rending melody expressing a passion that has no hope of earthly fulfillment:

65

And there is more tragedy in this unhappy triangle. The old king knows only too well that his wife was forced to break her engagement to his own son, and that she married him only for reasons of state, politics, to bring peace between France and Spain. He knows that her heart will never belong to him.

Again Verdi finds gripping musical expression for the lonely despair of the King. At the beginning of the third act, King Philip is alone in his palace, leaning over his papers, the candles burned down after a sleepless night. It is in this setting that he begins to sing about his frustrated love, and Verdi sets the mood by writing in the score *come trasognato,* as in a trance. The words, "Ella giammai m'amò," "she never loved me," are those of an unhappy man who realizes that he loves a woman who does not return his love, who never did return it!

FIL.

ELLA GIAM'AI MIA *M'È! NO, QUEL COR CHIUSO

M'È, AMOR PER ME NON HA, AMOR PER ME NON HA!

Against this dark background, the flame of another figure burns brightly, that of Rodrigo, Marchese di Posa. To Verdi, as to the original author, Schiller, this gentleman of great nobility was undoubtedly the most inspiring, the most appealing character in the entire story. Rodrigo is a fighter for freedom. He has made the cause of the suffering people of Flanders his own cause. He even sacrifices his own life for Don Carlo so that the Prince may rule one day as a gentler king over a happier country. Any champion of liberty was, of course, close to Verdi's freedom-loving heart.

Rodrigo is identified throughout the opera as a champion of liberty. And a great deal of this identification is made through music. The composer cannot use all the explanatory words of the poet to describe a character or a situation, so he gives the two friends, Rodrigo and Carlo, a ringing, expanded melody which is clearly identified with the ecstatic outcry, "Freedom!"

We hear this music for the first time at the end of the opening scene of the opera, when Don Carlo and Rodrigo swear to
live and die for the sake of liberty. The motive of liberty returns
in the final bars of the first scene in the second act. The Princess
Eboli has discovered Don Carlo's secret: it is the Queen, not
Princess Eboli, whom he loves. Eboli swears vengeance. Rodrigo,
determined to protect Carlo at all costs, first threatens to kill her,
but he suddenly checks himself. He throws away his dagger.
He has reached a decision. His own life does not count. In order
to protect Don Carlo from Eboli's vengeance, Rodrigo must
evolve a plan to insure Don Carlo's freedom, no matter what
the cost—which in this case means the sacrifice of his own life.

At this point of the opera, Don Carlo and Rodrigo actually become conspirators in the cause of liberty for Flanders. As the first step in Rodrigo's plan, he asks the prince to hand over to him secret political documents whose discovery means death to the bearer. They must not be found on Carlo. While the two friends leave the stage, the orchestra, triumphantly, announces that what Rodrigo has just done is for freedom's sake:

As the opera progresses, Rodrigo carries through his sacrifice. In the second scene of the second act, a climax is reached which results in a grave crisis between the two friends. Don Carlo appears before his father and asks to be sent to Flanders as the King's representative. The father, furious, jealous, and suspicious of his son, refuses. Don Carlo, now beyond control, draws his sword against his father, the King. The entire court freezes in terror; it is Rodrigo who steps forward, asks for Don Carlo's sword, and arrests him.

What a climax: the outburst of the King, the fury in the orchestra, and then sudden silence as Rodrigo steps forward and commands *"a me il ferro,"* "give me your sword." At this point we hear the liberty tune again, but this time a little slower as if played in the distance, as if coming deep out of the memory of Carlo, who, stunned, turns around unbelieving as he sees his friend disarming him and cries: "O heaven, you!" . . .

But this seeming act of betrayal is actually the supreme act of friendship. Rodrigo has not acted to save the King's life; he wants to save Carlo. The Prince goes to prison, but he lives, and Rodrigo continues on his self-chosen mission. His death alone, he believes, can absolve Don Carlo from any further suspicion, can liberate the Crown Prince from prison, can save his life

Finally, Rodrigo carries through his sacrifice. He sees to it that the incriminating papers are found in his own possession. Orders are given to kill him. And in the subsequent prison scene, as Rodrigo lies mortally wounded, the tune of liberty is heard for the last time. "Reach out your hand to me, Don Carlo," the faithful friend exclaims. "I shall die blissfully if my death saves for Spain a King and a redeemer. Don't forget me."

In the original play by Schiller, Rodrigo's sacrifice was in vain. In the final scene of the play, King Philip icily turned his son over to the punishing arm of the Inquisition. But Verdi has chosen a different ending. In the opera, Carlo is rescued at the very last moment, a strange rescue that has puzzled many a spectator. The mysterious figure of a monk suddenly steps out of the tomb of Charles the Fifth, in the cloister of San Giusto which serves as the background to the first and last scenes of the opera. The monk takes Carlo into the sanctuary of the tomb, and the Prince's life seems saved.

This rather ghostly friar had appeared earlier, in the first scene of the opera. At this time, when Don Carlo passed the monk, the young prince recognized his voice as the voice of his own grandfather, the great Emperor Charles the Fifth. When the monk appears in the last scene of the opera, he is again recognized by King Philip, by the other officers, and by the Grand Inquisitor. All are stunned by what they believe to be the ghost of Charles the Fifth. First the blind Inquisitor recognizes his voice.

Then the others identify the monk as the old Emperor.

Verdi took advantage of the persistent legend that Charles the Fifth, the mighty emperor on whose realm the sun never set, did not die at once after his abdication in favor of his son Philip but retired to the Cloister of St. Just. The story had it that he lived there in seclusion until his death.

Thus the monk is not a ghost but the old Emperor himself, who steps forward to save his grandson, at least according to Giuseppe Verdi. His deep affection for both Rodrigo and Don Carlo does not leave room for any other solution. If Don Carlo had been turned over to the Inquisitor as in Schiller's play, Rodrigo's sacrifice would have been in vain, his fight for justice and freedom would have gone unrewarded. Even after his hero, Rodrigo, is dead, Verdi reserves his most beautiful music for him. What could be more moving than the farewell sung by Queen Elisabeth and Don Carlo in this last duet, and the tribute they pay to their departed friend? "On the freed soil of Flanders," Don Carlo swears, "I will erect to Rodrigo a monument such as no king ever had on earth."

And Elisabeth dedicates a blossoming wreath of melody to Rodrigo's memory in one of Verdi's most beautiful phrases, as she sings: "The flowers of Paradise will smile on him."

I FIOR-DEL PARA-DI -SO A LUI SOR-RI-DE RAN-NO!

The dark clouds have been dispelled, the noise of swords, the voices of politics and religious controvresy have been silenced. Human tenderness can once more be felt through the tears that flow in Verdi's music.

Giuseppe Verdi, in Paris to discuss the first French performance of "La Forza del Destino," was persuaded by Emil Perrin, director of the Opera, to sign a contract on December 31, 1865, for a new five-act opera to be put into rehearsal the following July and produced in the French language the following November. The subject entrusted to the two libretttists, Camille du Locle and Francois Joseph Méry (1798-1865) was "Don Carlos," a vigorous romantic play written by Friedrich Schiller (1759-1805) in 1787. Troubled by a throat ailment, distressed by the

73

hostilities of the Austrians, and saddened by the fatal illness of his early patron and father-in-law, Antonio Barezzi, Verdi travelled to Nice, Genoa, home to Busseto, to Cauterets in the Pyrenees, and back to Paris before the music to "Don Carlo" was completed. After further delays the instrumentation was completed by November 10 and the opera achieved its première under Perrin's baton on March 11, 1867.

" 'Don Carlo' was not a success," Verdi wrote his friend Opprandino Arrivabene the following day, although Théophile Gautier waxed enthusiastic in the Moniteur, and the Temps reviewer felt that the composer "had enriched his style by resources borrowed from the French and German schools."

The cast was headed by Marie Sass as Elisabeth, her husband, Castelmary, playing the Monk. Jean-Baptiste Faure, composer of the popular Easter song, "The Palms," sang Rodrigo; Morère was the Don Carlo, Louis Obin, the King, while Messrs. David, Gaspard, and Mermant, respectively, sang the roles of the Grand Inquisitor, Count Lerma, and the Herald. Paulina Deligne Gueymard, daughter of the painter Lauters, sang Eboli, and Mme. Levieilly, Tebaldo.

Max Maretzek conducted the first American performance on April 12, 1877, at the New York Academy of Music under the management of Palmieri, whose wife, Maria, sang Queen Elisabeth. Mmes. Rastelli and Persiani were assigned the roles of Eboli and Tebaldo, while the Messrs. Celada, Bertolasi, Dal Negro, Garini, and Bacelli, personified Don Carlo, Rodrigo, Philip II, the Grand Inquisitor and the Monk.

"Don Carlo" was introduced to the Metropolitan Opera public on December 23, 1920, in the four-act version revised for La Scala by Verdi in 1884, with the Italian libretto prepared by Antonio Ghislanzoni. Gennaro Papi, who conducted, had made considerable cuts. Rosa Ponselle sang Elisabeth and was hailed

74

for the vocal gold of her voice but characterized by William J. Henderson of the Times as "neither queenly nor tear-compelling." Giovanni Martinelli was the Don Carlo; Margarete Matzenauer the Eboli, Giuseppe DeLuca the Rodrigo, and Adamo Didur the King. Other roles were taken by Louis D'Angelo (Inquisitor), Angelo Bada (Lerma and the Herald), William Gustafson (Monk), Ellen Dalossy (Tebaldo), Maria Savage (Countess d'Aremberg), and Marie Sundelius (Celestial Voice).

DON GIOVANNI

"DON GIOVANNI" has been the object of an amazing amount of discussion and study for a century and a half. Partisans of various points of view all agree that it is an extraordinary work, possibly the most perfect opera ever written, but they passionately disagree on what kind of a work it really is. Is it tragedy, comedy, or pure fantasy?

There are those who insist that it is the first romantic opera in the grand style, a serious, even tragic work. Listen to the arias of Donna Anna, Donna Elvira, and Don Ottavio, they exclaim. Can this be called comedy? Hear the poignant trio in the first scene, they elaborate further. Is the death of the Commendatore anything but tragedy?

The proponents of "Don Giovanni" as a lusty comedy have many good arguments for their contention. They quote the scenes involving Leporello. They mention the business of mistaken identity and the beating which the Don gives to Masetto.

Mozart himself seems to make plenty of musical fun with his three stage orchestras in the finale of the first act. One of them plays a Minuet.

Another plays a contradance.

A third plays the *Ländler*, which is a precursor of the waltz.

While some of the dance music is already in progress, the composer adds a realistic touch by making some of his instruments tune up, as a part of his musical joke.

Finally, Mozart combines the orchestras and we hear the three dance tunes simultaneously.

77

Yet at the other extreme from this light-hearted gaiety is the compelling supernatural aspect of "Don Giovanni." The statue of the dead Commendatore comes to life. At the close of the opera, avenging devils drag the hero down to eternal punishment. Mozart treats the fantastic elements with great seriousness and solemnity. He reserves the trombones for the exclusive purpose of characterizing the forces of supernatural retribution.

And the shivery passages in the woodwinds, which are heard in the overture and in the final scene, serve to illustrate the chilly gusts from beyond the grave.

Romantic drama, slapstick comedy, and supernatural tragedy mingle so closely in this work that it is impossible to determine which establishes its prevailing mood. Clowns, spooks, and human tears mingle in true Shakespearean fashion.

The miracle is that Mozart succeeded in mixing elements of farcical humor into a number of serious and supernatural scenes without in any way lessening their poignancy or eeriness. Thus, Donna Elvira's emotional turmoil, in the trio of the second act, sounds completely convincing and sincere in spite of the coarse and heartless comedy of disguises which takes place under her balcony. In the graveyard scene, the feeling of mystery and awe

79

is not lessened one iota by Leporello's loutish fears and shaking knees.

In the last scene, the composer pulls off perhaps the greatest stunt in the opera by combining all three elements simultaneously: Don Giovanni suggests the tragedy of man, the Commendatore makes his ghostly visitation, and Leporello cowers under the table.

This combination of genres, which seemed so puzzling to nineteenth-century opera lovers, need not trouble anyone today. It has become rather obvious to present-day Mozart connoisseurs that the great Austrian moved with equal ease in all types and styles of music. Other Mozart works, such as "The Magic Flute," show a similar mixture of fantastic and comic elements. The astonishing thing is that, with all his freedom of approach, Mozart was nevertheless completely satisfied to follow certain conventions of the eighteenth century which have since been discarded. The entire action of "Don Giovanni" for instance, unrolls within the twenty-four hours demanded by the theatrical usage of the time. Some writers have pointed out that the statue of the Commendatore could not have been constructed and erected overnight, but they overlook the fact that it could easily have been fashioned years before to grace the burial place of the Commendatore's family!

The only thing which needed to be of recent origin is the inscription on the pedestal of the statue, and that could have been done in a few hours unless it is simply another magic trick evoked by the supernatural might of avenging providence!

Mozart spoke to his contemporaries in the language of their own time, and yet he was able to weld the human, the comic, and the supernatural into one of the world's greatest lyric dramas. Such was his sovereign mastery in the art of wedding music to the theater.

The legend of Don Juan Tenorio y Salazar of Seville was first recorded in a play entitled "El Burlador de Seville, y Combidado de Pietra" ("The Mocker of Seville and the Stone Guest") by the Spanish monk Gabriel Tellez, who published the work in 1630 under the pseudonym Tirso de Molina. The subject was popular among seventeenth century playwrights, notably Molière, who brought out a new version, "Le Festin de Pierre," in 1665, while other variants were written by Carlo Goldoni (1760) and Giovanni Bertati (1775). The latter was freely used by Lorenzo da Ponte in providing the libretto of "Don Giovanni" for Wolfgang Amadeus Mozart (1756-1791).

The opera was commissioned in January, 1787, by Pasquale Bondini, impresario of a local Italian opera company in Prague, where Mozart's "Abduction from the Seraglio" and later his "The Marriage of Figaro" had both been enthusiastically received. Librettist and composer worked together briefly in Vienna, assisted by the notorious Casanova de Seingalt. In September, Mozart set out for Prague, lodging with an attractive singer, the former Josepha Hambacher, and her husband, the musician Franz Duschek, who provided him with a congenial atmosphere at their suburban villa. Da Ponte joined them on October 8, and on October 29, after several delays occasioned by the illness of the singers concerned, "Don Giovanni" was introduced at the National Theater.

The title role was performed by Luigi Bassi, a baritone of twenty-two, who complained that he had "no big aria to sing." The Zerlina was Katerina Bondini, wife of the impresario. Teresa Saporti sang Donna Anna, and Caterina Micelli, Donna Elvira. Antonio Baglioni was the Don Ottavio, while Giuseppe Lolli performed both Masetto and the Commendatore, a situation which necessitated the introduction of demons during the

81

last scene so that the basso could change his costume for the coming ensemble.

A few days after the first performance, which Mozart himself conducted from the piano, the Prague Oberpostamtszeitung published a brief but comprehensive review on the subject: "Connoisseurs and musicians say that nothing like it has ever before been produced in Prague."

"Don Giovanni" reached the United States on May 27, 1825, presented at the Park Theater by the renowned Spanish tenor Manuel Garcia and his troupe, with a French pianist, M. Etienne, as conductor. Garcia the elder sang the title role, deserting his usual *tessitura* and hiding the vocal ravages of his advancing years by his extraordinary skill. His daughter Maria, who later married the elderly French scapegrace Eugène Malibran, was described as "brilliant, beautiful, and amiable," in the role of Zerlina, by da Ponte, then resident in New York. Mme. Garcia sang Donna Elvira, and Manuel Garcia, Jr., Leporello. M. Milon was dubbed "utterly inadequate" for the role of Ottavio by the critic of the weekly Albion, and Mme. Barbieri, commended for her "sweet and clear" scale, was judged less successful as Donna Anna than in other roles. Carlo Anghissimi sang both Masetto and the Commendatore.

Auguste Vianesi conducted the Metropolitan première of "Don Giovanni" on November 28, 1883, with Giuseppe Kaschmann in the title role. The three women, Emmy Fursch-Madi as Donna Anna, Christine Nilsson as Donna Elvira, and Marcella Sembrich as Zerlina, were praised by Mr. Krehbiel in the Tribune for their excellent work, but the instrumental musicians "made a sad mess of the finale of the first act." Roberto Stagno sang Don Giovanni, and the other roles were filled by Giovanni Mirabella (Leporello), Achille Augier (the Commendattore), and Baldassare Corsini (Masetto).

ELEKTRA

"ELEKTRA," although written as a single act without intermission, is a complete operatic event in itself. It is such a towering tragedy, a work of such fiery passion and tremendous power, that one could hardly want any other opera on the same bill, regardless of its merits.

Fate takes its irrevocable, terrible course in one breath-taking sweep; Strauss knew just what he meant when he failed to provide an intermission: there is no place for the drama to stop.

It is significant that Strauss does not call "Elektra" an opera. He calls it simply a tragedy, and it remains today one of the great eternal tragedies of mankind. Sophocles and Euripides wrote their own "Elektras" some 2,500 years ago. And the libretto which Hugo von Hofmannsthal wrote for Richard Strauss, while modern in its psychological—one would almost say psycho-analytical—implications, still follows the ancient story very closely.

Elektra and her family come out of one of humanity's oldest and most celebrated classics, "Homer's Iliad." Elektra's father was Agamemnon, the king who led the Greek armies in the Trojan war. When Agamemnon returned home he was killed by his wife, Klytemnestra, with the help of Aegisthus, Klytemnestra's lover. Agamemnon's young son, Orestes, was then sent away by Klytemnestra and her new husband, Aegisthus, but both of them trembled at the thought that Orestes might return to avenge the death of his father. Elektra had also been a child when the murder of Agamemnon was committed, but she had never forgotten, and through all these years she had thought only of vengeance. This, then, is the horrifying background for the Strauss-Hoffmansthal tragedy.

As the curtain opens we see the courtyard outside the palace of Klytemnestra. The royal household, down to the humblest servant, hates Elektra, despises her, fears her. Whoever dares to take her side is punished. Klytemnestra, her aging mother, is tormented by fear and the memories of the past. She pleads in vain with Elektra for a single sign of love, a gesture of forgiveness; but Elektra waits only for the hour of retribution. And now, after all these years of waiting and scheming and hating, the hour has arrived. Orestes, the exiled brother, returns at last. The mother is slain. Her husband Aegisthus, returning from the fields, follows her in sudden violent death, also at the hand of Orestes. At last Agamemnon, Elektra's hero, her father, the beloved shadow, is avenged, and she breaks out in a horrible dance of triumph till she also collapses, dead, consumed by a dark passion and a joy too violent, too unnatural even for so strong and unbending a character as this strange child of a great father.

Although King Agamemnon is dead and does not appear in the opera, he actually dominates the action and even the music. At the very beginning of the opera his name is spelled out, simply and powerfully. There is no overture to the work. The curtain rises immediately on a short unforgettable phrase:

In these four notes, derived from a simple triad, the name of the dead hero, Agamemnon, is announced in majesty and striking simplicity, like a coat of arms on the mighty portal of a castle.

The simplicity of the opening bars must not mislead us. As the drama of dark hatred and violent passion unfolds, Strauss translates it through some of the most complicated and nerve-wracking music in all operatic literature. This music penetrates deeply into the hearts and minds of his characters: Elektra, who has waited so long for the hour of vengeance, and Klytemnestra, who disintegrates in body and spirit, haunted by unspeakable fears, by nightmares which have never before been expressed so horrifyingly in music. As Strauss himself once said, with perhaps more truth than modesty, this music goes to the very limit of what human ears can endure!

The composer must have been well aware of the overwhelming effect his music would produce. In order to counterbalance that whirling impact of passionate sounds which engulf singers and listeners alike, he has introduced a number of very simple and easily recognizable themes to portray the characters of the opera.

We have already mentioned Agamemnon's theme. Soon after the curtain rises, another Agamemnon motive, this time the motive of his ghost, is introduced. It appears when Elektra talks about her dead father who returns, as she puts it, "with eyes wide open, glaring at the house, with slow relentless steps and vengeful eyes."

85

This is pure, disembodied rhythm, skipping from the lowest bass to the highest treble like an immense, all-pervading spirit.

Elektra's own motive is also monumental, but clear, simple, precise.

Although at first the melodies are simple, they soon become soaked in harmonies of utmost deliberate ugliness. Nothing helps more to create that astonishing effect of almost superhuman horror than these constant waves of nightmarish harmonic terror that seem to drown the human beings that are caught in this tragic maelstrom.

Strauss takes an innocent formation of four notes, a formation perfectly well-known in conventional harmony, technically called the third inversion of a seventh chord. First we have the simple dominant seventh chord:

Then the inversion of the dominant seventh:

Now listen to what the composer does to this innocuous sounding chord:

86

Here is the horrifying sound of murder—foul, terrible, inescapable murder. This mood is achieved by adding just one note to the chord—a note a perfect fifth lower than its normal bass.

The lowest note of a chord is its most sensitive point, and that is what Strauss attacks. In a very real sense the chord is killed, murdered, and this murdered chord is symbolic also of the axe with which Agamemnon was slain, the very axe which Elektra has buried in the courtyard to preserve for her day of terrible retribution.

This murder chord sounds again and again in the score whenever the "butchering" (as Elektra calls it), the murder of her father Agamemnon, is mentioned or described. The murder chord sometimes creeps into some of the important musical themes, and virtually murders them whenever such necessity suits the composer's purpose and helps him emphasize a particular dramatic development. Here is the music that accompanies Elektra's first appearance in the opera:

Elektra's theme is accompanied by the murder chord, a tortured, deformed phrase which seems to say: "Look what the murder of her father did to this once so beautiful child, how fate has transformed this proud human being, a princess, into a tormented, bloodthirsty Harpy."

The score is full of similar musical descriptions, such as the whipping sounds of the orchestra when one of the serving maids, the only one that dares to defend Elektra, is punished early in the opera.

Musical illustrations of dramatic events abound in the score. The galloping horse, for example, is hurriedly dispatched as a messenger to call Aegisthus from the fields when the news of Orestes' supposed death is heard.

The eerie glow of the magic stones that hang from Klytemnestra's neck and arms, the stones which she superstitiously believes will drive away the peril that threatens her is suggested in music.

At the climax of the scene between Elektra and Klytemnestra, when Elektra tells her mother that she longs for vengeance and describes how she will hunt her *down the steps* of the palace to her doom, the orchestra runs *down a chromatic scale*.

Sometimes Strauss' superb technique carries these minute illustrations to the border line of musical hysteria. When Elektra warns her terrified mother that she will hunt her like a hound, the orchestra describes the barkings of dogs pitilessly pursuing their prey.

Not all the music of "Elektra," however, is of such lurid nature. Chrysothemis, Elektra's gentle sister, represents the normal, the average. She is the innocent, uncomprehending, and bewildered member of this family, caught in the relentless and tragic turmoil. Her only aspiration is to free herself of the surrounding evil and pursue a placid and serene existence. Some of Chrysothemis' music is so lush and romantically melodious that the composer was occasionally accused of cheapening the score.

Another example of mellifluous tenderness is found in the supremely moving recognition scene between Elektra and Orestes. Here Elektra relaxes and expresses overwhelming joy that the brother she believed lost forever has now returned to fulfill his predestined obligation to revenge.

Audiences are surprised to hear such soothing, melodic loveliness—these sudden valleys of beauty in the bleak, violent mountains of the score. But, with his unfailing theatrical intuition, Strauss knew precisely what he was doing. The unrelieved tortures of mother and daughter, the horrors of the story, would probably be more than audiences could endure without these contrasting melodic passages. Furthermore, against the background of these mellower and lighter sections of the score, the surrounding sounds of horror make an even more ferocious impression.

Elektra's story has fascinated people for thousands of years. Nothing but the most tumultuous music could do it justice. When the librettist and the composer tackled the story of Elektra, they touched the garments of Euripides, Aeschylus and Sophocles, daring to follow where giants had roamed thousands of years before. Time alone will measure their stature.

"Elektra," the first opera by Richard Strauss (1864-1949) for which Hugo von Hofmannsthal (1874-1929) provided a libretto, takes its theme from the dramas of Aeschylus, Sophocles and Euripides but invests the epic myth with new psychopathic overtones. Characterized by Wallace Brockway and Herbert Weinstock as "a tragic masterpiece of the very first order," "Elektra" remains "as shattering, as moving, as profound in terror, as on the night of its première."

This took place on January 25, 1909, at the Royal Opera House in Dresden, under the baton of Fritz von Schuch. After the success of "Salome" the publishers insisted on getting the new score from Strauss page by page, as it was written, paying $27,000 for the privilege. Within four weeks of the première "Elektra" was produced in Munich, Frankfort and Berlin.

Annie Krull created the title role in Dresden with Ernestine Schumann-Heink as Klytemnestra. The famous contralto related that when the conductor, out of regard for the singers, subdued the orchestra at rehearsal, Strauss declared "But, my dear Schuch, louder, louder the orchestra; I can still hear the voice of Frau Heink." She resigned after a single performance. Margarete Siems sang Chrysothemis; Karl Perron, Orestes, and Johannes Sembach, Aegisthus, the latter coming to the Metropolitan five years later for Wagnerian roles.

The rest of the cast comprised Julius Buttlitz (Foster Father), Gertrud Sachse (Confidant), Elisabeth Boehm von Endert (Trainbearer), Franz Nebuschka (Old Servant), Fritz Soot (Young Servant), Riza Eibenschütz (Overseer). The serving women were Franciska Bender-Schäfer, Magdalene Seebe, Irma Tervani, Anna Zoder, and Minnie Rast.

Oscar Hammerstein paid Strauss $10,000 for the American rights to "Elektra" and $18,000 in advance royalties, doubling the price of seats at the United States première, which took place on February 1, 1910, at the Manhattan Opera House. A French translation by Henri Gauthier-Villars was used and seven presentations were conducted by Henriquez De La Fuente. Mariette Mazarin's blazing passion and maniacal intensity as Elektra proved so taxing that the French soprano fainted while taking a curtain call. "A figure of strange and haunting power," said Richard Aldrich in the Times. Jeanne Gerville-Réache, a pupil of Pauline Viardot-Garcia, found, like Schumann-Heink, that one Klytemnestra was enough, and withdrew after the first performance. Alice Baron sang Chrysothemis; Gustave Huberdeau was the Orestes; M. Duffault was Aegisthus; M. Nicolay the Foster Father; M. Venturini the Young Servant; M. Scott the Old Servant; Mlle. Desmond the Confidant; Mlle. Taty-Lango the Overseer; Mlle. Johnstone the Trainbearer, while the Serving Women were the Mmes. Alice Gentle, Severina, Milda, Walter-Villa, and Duchène. "The performance was one of astonishing excellence and power," wrote the Times reviewer, stressing the fluency of the orchestra, but the *mot juste* was voiced by a colleague, Arthur Farwell, who called "Elektra" "the marriage of horror and beauty."

"Elektra" did not reach the Metropolitan until December 3, 1932, when it was conducted by Artur Bodanzky in what Wm. J. Henderson described in the Sun as a "masterful" manner. Lawrence Gilman in the Herald Tribune stated that Gertrud Kappel accomplished "an earnestly conceived embodiment of the heroine" but was "deplorably miscast." Praising Friedrich Schorr as Orestes and Rudolf Laubenthal as Aegisthus, Mr. Gilman accorded little musicianship to Göta Ljungberg as Chrysothemis and liked Karin Branzell's singing of Klytemnestra better than her impersonation. Siegfried Tappolet was the Foster Father; Arnold Gabor and Marek Windheim the old and young servants; Grace Divine and Pearl Besuner the Confidant and Trainbearer respectively. The Serving Women, under Dorothee Manski as Overseer, were Doris Doe, Ina Bourskaya, Philine Falco, Helen Gleason, and Margaret Halstead.

FAUST

EVEN those who hear the opera "Faust" for the first time may be surprised that so much of the music sounds familiar. Whether aware of it or not, most people know a great deal of Gounod's "Faust:" they have sung it in school, they have heard it in restaurants, and they have listened to amateurs of varying degrees of competence tackle the arias.

While most great operas can boast of songs that have become universally popular, few of them can produce such a long list of perennial favorites as "Faust": Marguerite's "Jewel Song," the love duet in the garden scene, Valentin's farewell aria, the waltz chorus, the "Soldiers' Chorus," Faust's own cavatina: "Salut, demeure"; Méphistophélès' "Serenade," his song of the Golden Calf, and the famous trio in prison!

It seems that familiarity is an almost indispensable factor in the enjoyment of music, and when people say they know what they like, they are actually saying that they like what they know!

"Faust" is so full of melody it seems hard to realize that when the opera was first produced musicians and critics complained it wasn't melodious enough. It was said to be too learned, too full of instrumental complexities.

From the vantage point of today, we are inclined to smile at the obtuseness of our great-grandfathers. Still, we must remember that the wisdom of hindsight is easily come by. It is highly probable that later generations will love certain aspects of today's modern music which some of our listeners find rather hard to enjoy!

As far as a true estimate of "Faust" is concerned, perhaps in a different way we make almost as much of a mistake as Gounod's contemporary critics. If they found the opera too complex to be appreciated, we find it so pleasantly simple that we are apt to underestimate its merits as operatic writing.

Actually, "Faust" is a good deal more than just a collection of delightful melodies. The music serves a dramatic purpose, which it is artfully constructed to fulfill. One has only to look at the writing of such individual parts as that of Méphistophélès, for instance, to see how careful Gounod was to be dramatically appropriate as well as melodious and tuneful.

The reason Méphistophélès' music has a special subtlety is that the gentleman himself is an unusually complicated, chameleon-like character. The Devil, Mephisto, is presented in "Faust" as the Great Corrupter. His purpose is to lead members of the human race to perdition and eternal damnation. He seduces men and women from the path of virtue by playing on their weaknesses and encouraging them in their wicked inclinations. He is devilishly brilliant and adjusts himself cleverly to every situation. This adaptability is reflected in his music in an interesting fashion.

First he chooses to appear to Faust in the guise of a debonair and elegant young man about town. He is everything that Faust is not, and he knows that it is exactly this quality which will make the aged philosopher a more likely prospect for temptation. This quality of urbane elegance is present in Mephisto's music: "Don't you like my get-up?" he asks Faust. "A sword at my side, a plume in my cap, a well-filled purse, a velvet cloak on my shoulder: in short a true gentleman!"

He is a gay young blade, if I ever heard one!

When he wants to join the rowdy crew of students and soldiers in the scene at the fair he easily adapts himself to their very different mood. As a matter of fact, he uses a time-honored device to break into a jovial crowd by saying in effect: "Did you fellows ever hear the one about . . . ?" Then he sings the rowdy song of the Golden Calf which is just the sort of noisy tune the students and soldiers would appreciate.

When he is dealing with gullible old Marthe, he takes still another tack. In order to facilitate Faust's flirtation with Marguerite, the Devil so befuddles Marthe with implied promises of marriage that she can no longer serve as an efficient chaperone. When he presses his attention on her, he does it with an obvious and coarse musical ardor, just the approach that will work with Marthe, of course!

95

Now compare the Devil's unctuous, almost pious tone of voice when he addresses Marguerite in the church scene, with the offensive, jeering, cynical impertinences of his Serenade. This contrast makes perfectly good sense as soon as we recollect that although Mephisto is ostensibly serenading Marguerite, his ultimate intention is to be heard by Valentin, Marguerite's brother. The more nastily suggestive his song, the more certain the Devil is, not only of provoking Valentin into a duel with Faust, but also of inducing that worthy soldier to discard the holy medal, that gift from Marguerite against which the evil magic of the Devil would be powerless! The scurrilous innuendo of the Serenade does the trick: Valentin tosses away the medal, and the way is open for Mephisto to accomplish still another of his nefarious goals, to make a murderer out of Faust!

Thus, Méphistophélès adapts himself to the situation in furtherance of his evil aims, and, invariably, the evil of his nature is clearly evident in his music.

96

When the Devil cannot accomplish his goal by playing on the weaknesses of his victim, he does not hesitate to use other methods. Marguerite's innocence and purity are such that Mephisto has to resort to rather dubious means, such as magic jewels and evil emanations of enchanted flowers. It is no accident, therefore, that while in the end Faust's soul becomes the property of Mephisto, Marguerite manages to escape amid the jubilant strains of the Angels' *"sauvée"*—"saved!"

Familiar melodies are unquestionably an invaluable asset to any musical composition, but we must not lose sight of the fact that Gounod has brought to bear a vigorous dramatic imagination as well as a musical one in the creation of "Faust." The result is a work which remains a perennial favorite.

Charles François Gounod (1818-1893) told Léon Carvalho, who was then director of the Paris Théâtre Lyrique and who in 1856 first suggested "Faust" as an operatic theme to the composer, that he "had had that in his stomach" for many years. The next day Gounod met the librettists, Michel Carré (1819-1872) and Jules Barbier (1825-1901) who had previously offered to Meyerbeer a libretto based on the epic which Goethe had written between 1808 and 1831.

In 1857 Gounod suffered a breakdown, associated with the feverish heat to which his temperament rose in the creation of the masterpiece. Refused by the Paris Opéra, the work was somewhat altered to meet Carvalho's demands for the Lyrique, the Soldiers' Chorus being added in rehearsal from another opera by Gounod, "Ivan the Terrible."

At the première, on March 19, 1859, the title role was taken by a mediocre tenor, Giuseppe Barbot. The composer was pleased with Balanqué, who sang Méphistophélès, and Caroline Miolan-Carvalho, the wife of the director, who sang Marguerite. The baritone, Osmond Reynald, was Valentin; Amélie Faivre, Siébel; Cibot, Wagner; and Duclos, Marthe. M. Deloffre conducted.

German was the language of the American première, which took place in Philadelphia under the auspices of the Theodor Habelmann Company on November 18, 1863. Marie Frederici was the Marguerite and Franz Himmer the Faust, with Graff as Méphistophélès, H. Steinecke as Valentin, and Johannsen Siebel. Karl Anschütz, former Arion conductor, was on the podium.

When "Faust" opened the inaugural season at the Metropolitan Opera House on October 22, 1883, Italian was the language used by the cast and conductor, Auguste Vianesi. Christine Nilsson, the "Margherita," had developed "dignity and nobility" in the art which New Yorkers had known for some thirteen years, according to Henry Krehbiel of the Tribune. Italo Campanini only occasionally demonstrated his "old-time sweetness" and "manly ring" as Faust, in the words of the same critic. Louise Lablache, replacing her mother, "did her work cleverly" as Marthe, while Sofia Scalchi "did the most artistic singing of the evening" as Siébel. Giuseppe Del Puente, the first American Alfio and Lescaut, sang Valentin; Franco Novara (Frank Nash) was the Méphistophélès, and Ludovico Contini the Wagner.

LA FORZA DEL DESTINO

"LA FORZA DEL DESTINO," or "The Power of Destiny," is a title which indicates one difference from most of the other Verdi operas. While the score provides true Verdi music: dramatic, lyrical, emotional from beginning to end, the story is unlike any other the composer has set, and the clue is in the title. In this opera it is not the soprano or the tenor, not the mezzo or the baritone who plays the leading role. The motivating device is an intangible force, destiny itself.

The play from which Verdi adapted this opera was entitled "Don Alvaro" and subtitled "The Power of Destiny." But rather than use the name of Don Alvaro or of one of the other characters for the title of his opera, Verdi used the subtitle, "La Forza del Destino." Destiny plays the lead.

Most of Verdi's operas, which he named after a hero or heroine, are human dramas of great intensity and subtlety. The composer carefully develops human characters. He takes pains to convey their believable reactions in any given situation. But in "The Power of Destiny" the three leading figures, Leonora, her brother Don Carlo, and her lover Don Alvaro, are hopelessly caught in a series of events over which they have no control. Weird coincidences, strange accidents ruin their best intentions. They are trapped by developments which they could never have foreseen, let alone forestalled.

Even before the curtain rises we are already forewarned by the orchestra. The very first measures of the overture introduce the central theme of the work. Not a person is portrayed, not a situation, not an emotion, nor the pastoral music of a landscape. The theme we hear is rigid, cold, superhuman, like fate itself.

The music continues at once to describe the vain struggle of the victims as they try to escape:

The opening scene starts in a simple, ordinary manner. A doting father, about to retire, bids his loving daughter good night with much tenderness and affection. Shortly after Leonora's father leaves her, Don Alvaro arrives to carry her away on their carefully planned elopement. Here destiny makes its first cruel appearance. Just what prompted Leonora's father to return at that very moment? Luckless Don Alvaro tries desperately to prove his honorable intentions, but the enraged father refuses to listen to his pleas and explanations. "Take my life, then," Alvaro cries. "Your daughter is innocent." The young man throws his weapon to the floor, and fate, malicious as ever in this opera, pulls the trigger. The pistol goes off; the Marquis is killed, and we have witnessed the only accidental death in all operatic literature!

Another unusual circumstance is the fact that the two lovers, soprano and tenor, are irrevocably separated after this first scene and do not appear together again until the end of the opera. To compensate for this enforced separation, Verdi gives these two unhappy creatures an unusually moving and beautiful love scene, not the common variety of tender conversations and caresses, but a tense and passionate love duet, ending in an impetuous *allegro brillante* filled with hurry and turmoil:

There is a special poignancy in their words repeated so many times—"fate will never divide us," for a few moments later fate divides them forever.

Don Alvaro is one of Verdi's most interesting heroes. Child of

101

a noble Inca mother and a Spanish rebel father, a man of noble and generous nature, the unfortunate Alvaro has the finest and most honorable intentions throughout the opera: he wants to marry Leonora, be respectful to the old Marquis, friendly with Leonora's brother, Don Carlo. It all comes to naught! It is as if some ancient god of the Incas had chosen Alvaro to destroy the family of Calatrava in symbolic retribution for the Spaniards' conquest of the New World. As a result of his unhappy experiences, Alvaro develops a streak of melancholy which to us is particularly fascinating, since melancholy is an unusual mood for a hero of Verdi. The melody Verdi fashioned to portray this state of mind is one of the most haunting he composed; it has a frustrated, almost tired contour and is heard on several occasions in the second act:

Convinced that Leonora is dead, our hero goes to war and here again meets a queer twist of fate. Don Carlo and Don Alvaro, unknown to each other, serve in the Spanish army in Italy. Don Carlo's life is saved by none other than Alvaro, whom he has vowed to kill. The men, unaware of their true identities, swear eternal friendship.

This third person of the drama, Don Carlo, knows neither frustrations nor hesitations. He has sworn to avenge his father's death and the dishonor of his family. He acts according to the inviolable Spanish code of honor, and so he relentlessly pursues both Don Alvaro and his own sister Leonora, whom he regards as a depraved accomplice of the murderer.

Exposed to the deadly loathing of Don Carlo, Alvaro decides to withdraw from the world and devote his life to Christian service in a remote monastery. Again Verdi creates a special theme to illustrate Don Alvaro's self-sacrificing humility:

We have heard this melody in the Prelude to the opera, and have guessed from the very beginning that the shield of renunciation would not protect Don Alvaro from the storms of inimical fate.

The monastery of Alvaro's choice turns out to be the very one where, under the guise of a hermit, Leonora has found refuge and protection in a cave. Don Carlo finally finds Don Alvaro at his monastery and provokes him to a duel which leads both men into the vicinity of Leonora's cave. Here the mortally wounded Don Carlo succeeds in killing his sister before expiring himself.

103

It is a commonplace of theatrical craft that accidents and coincidences weaken the believability of the story and antagonize the spectator. The plot of "The Force of Destiny" has not escaped criticism on that score. We must remember, however, that here, for once, these alleged weaknesses represent a necessary and unavoidable ingredient. These strange and unpredictable turns of events become the very tools with which the real protagonist of the drama, destiny, crushes the lives of its victims.

Giuseppe Verdi signed a contract for a new opera with the direction of the Imperial Theater in St. Petersburg on June 3, 1861. For two years the composer had been interested in the character of Don Alvaro, the hero of an historical play by Don Angel de Saavedra, Duke of Rivas (1835), which had introduced the Romantic movement to the Spanish stage. By 1860 Verdi had already begun the composition of the opera, which he completed by January, 1862. He spent the summer months orchestrating it. The libretto was the work of Francesco Maria Piave (1810-1876), who for once proved so inept in his early revisions of the text that Verdi replaced him in 1868 by Antonio Ghislanzoni, the librettist of "Aïda."

The première of the opera, which took place on November 10, 1862, at the St. Petersburg Opera, was "a great success," according to a letter written by Mme. Verdi a few days later. The Emperor, who was prevented by illness from attending the opera until its fourth performance, bestowed the Commander's Cross of the Imperial Order of St. Stanislas on the composer. The Russian correspondent of the French magazine, Nord, found "many fresh and new ideas scattered in this scholarly work" and commended the elevation of the style and the originality of the choruses.

The first cast was led by the great Roman tenor Enrico Tamberlik, whose trill was renowned. His friend, Francesco Graziani, for whom Verdi wrote the part of Rodrigo, sang Don Carlo on this occasion. Constance Nantier-Didiée, for whom Gounod added an aria to Siébel's role in "Faust," was the first Preziosilla. The renowned bass, Alberto De Bassini, sang Fra Melitone, and Gian Francesco Angelini, already famous at the age of thirty-two, was the Guardiano. Carolina Barbot, from the Apollo Theater in Rome, was the Leonora.

"La Forza del Destino" reached the United States on February 24, 1865, when it was conducted by Carl Bergmann at the New York Academy of Music, earning the description of the Times reviewer as "an opera of fine proportions, not overcharged with tunes." Carlotta Carozzi-Zucchi, who had made a hit as the "Trovatore" Leonora the previous October, sang the heroine's role with the beautiful Kate Duckworth Morensi, a pupil of Adelaide Phillipps, as Preziosilla. Bernardo Massimiliani, who had been engaged for the leading roles in "Trovatore" and "Lucia" by Max Maretzek, was the Don Alvaro, while Domenico Bellini was promoted from a minor role in "Trovatore" to sing Padre Guardiano. Dubreuil was the Melitone.

By the time that "La Forza del Destino" reached the Metropolitan stage on November 15, 1918, the Times critic decided that, far from being "not overcharged with tunes," it was "absolutely crammed, musically speaking." Rosa Ponselle made her debut on this occasion in the role of Leonora, proving "a dramatic soprano of splendid potentialities" to James Huneker of the same paper. Enrico Caruso's interpretation of Alvaro's music was judged the "highlight of the performance" by the same reviewer. Giuseppe De Luca sang Don Carlo, with the famous Spanish basso José Mardones as Guardiano. Alice Gentle made "an inconspicuous debut" as Preziosilla. Thomas Chalmers, who later withdrew to the spoken stage, sang Melitone; Marie Mattfeld was Curra; Louis D'Angelo, the Marquis; Paolo Ananian, the Alcade; and Vincenzo Reschiglian, the Surgeon.

LA GIOCONDA

OF ALL the operas in the standard repertory, "La Gioconda" most truly merits the epithet "grand" in the familiar term "grand opera." Everything about Ponchielli's opera is grandiose. It is a spectacle of great splendor and lavish display, with large masses of participants both in the pit and on stage. It is replete with startling color, variety of costumes, and astonishing scenic effects.

The conception of opera as a magnificent pageant is largely associated with the Paris of the second quarter of the nineteenth century, and is closely attached to the name of Meyerbeer. Most of the effects which in our day have been exploited by Hollywood were anticipated by Meyerbeer in "Les Huguenots," "Le Prophète," and "L' Africaine." Roller-skating ballets, bathing beauties, startling scenic phenomena, and the employment of a veritable army of singers and supernumeraries are the hallmarks of the Meyerbeerian grand opera.

The very descriptions of the scenes in "La Gioconda" indicate that Ponchielli fell heir to the tastes of his predecessor. Act I is laid in "the grand courtyard of the ducal palace in Venice, decorated for festivities." The third act plays in "a magnificent hall in the 'House of Gold,' splendidly adorned." Even though the fourth act takes us only to "the vestibule of a palace in ruins," the lagoon and the square of St. Mark are seen at the rear "brilliantly illuminated."

The specifications of the "Gioconda" wardrobe are equally extravagant. There are thirty-six richly brocaded costumes with fur-trimmed mantles to adorn the Venetian noblemen and officials; forty-five peasant costumes, some of wool and some of cotton, in different colors; twelve sailor uniforms with blue pants; red-and-white striped shirts, blue capes, red caps and leggings. Forty-five court ladies' dresses are specified of velvet or brocade, some with velvet mantles and gold necklaces with stones; twenty-six ballet costumes are required, some with sequins and of variegated colors. There must be four pages in green and twelve additional peasant costumes, and so on *ad infinitum.*

Nor is this splendor confined to the spectacle which is afforded the eye. The music faithfully reflects the glamor. In the first act the gaiety and abandon of the carnival masqueraders is denoted in the *furlana,* a gay and lively dance.

In the third act the rustling of the silks, brocades, and velvets of Alvise's guests can almost be heard in the stately dance which ushers them in.

The luxury of these patrician costumes is particularly effective after the relative simplicity of those of the sailors, fishermen, and rustic maidens in the preceding scene.

In addition to the pictorial effect Ponchielli created in the score and the sumptuousness of the scenery and costumes he commanded, the master evoked the subtlest techniques of the lighting department to further his illusion.

In the second act it is obvious that Enzo and Laura cannot set sail and flee from Venice until the moon sets and darkness protects them. Midway in their duet they remark that the moon is beginning to sink:

It then devolves upon the electrician to time its descent with imperceptible slowness so that it will disappear below the horizon just in time.

Meanwhile both clouds in the sky and ripples on the water are being projected by means of revolving disk machines, while the burning of the ship requires the use of every available device involving electricity and steam.

But "La Gioconda" is not only grand opera, it is also the perfect melodrama, a term defined by Webster as "a kind of drama, commonly romantic and sensational, with both song and instrumental interludes." We must certainly admit that the romantic element in "Gioconda" is put on with a heavy brush. To begin with, the authors selected for the locale what is possibly the most romantic city in the world, Venice; for the time, the seventeenth century, a period never excelled for its romantic pageantry and glamor. The sensationalism of the melodrama, as Webster defines it, is apparent in the exaggerated and over-drawn emotions of the leading characters. They all get ample opportunity to display their feelings without the slightest inhibition. Gioconda in particular has every chance to shine in an almost unbelievable array of emotional heroics. The tenor, Enzo, is no shrinking violet: a prince disguised as a sailor, defending a street singer's mother, trying to escape with another's man's wife, and confronting the husband in his own palace! Here is a swashbuckling character of the first water! It would be hard to find a more evil and malicious villain than the Inquisition spy Barnaba, although Alvise, Laura's husband, if to some extent justified in his grudge against the tenor, Enzo, indulges in a form of revenge which is drastic, to say the least! Killing (as he thinks) his own wife and then flaunting the murder to his assembled guests comes close to matching all of Barnaba's operatic delinquencies.

In this age of underplayed passions and brittle drawing-room comedies, it is refreshing to be exposed to the unblushing heroics of "La Gioconda." Its blood-and-thunder, cloak-and-dagger melodrama cries for the grandest, most eloquent music, which is just what we are granted from beginning to the end. One could almost suppose that Ponchielli and Boïto first wrote a group of arias and duets to express all sorts of variations on love, hate, and jealousy, and finally had to devise a plot to string them together. In the second act, for example, the island does not turn out to be deserted after all. Otherwise we could not have the exciting *marinesca*, the mariner's chorus—which involves the crew of Enzo's ship, not to mention all kinds of men, women, and children who throng the shore, while our perpetual villain, Barnaba, sings his own fisherman's ballad.

Mysteriously Enzo manages to clear the stage in a matter of seconds to be alone for his great aria, "Cielo e mar," a song of love and hope and the happy life ahead with Laura. The most romantic moment in the opera occurs in the ensuing duet between the two lovers, Enzo and Laura, alone together for the first time, happy in each other's arms at last.

But, at this point, Gioconda herself still has many unexpressed emotions waiting to be voiced in song. Soon she bursts forth from her mysterious hiding-place under the prow of the ship, dagger in hand, ready for battle, a perfect occasion for a magnificent encounter between the soprano and the mezzo-soprano. This scene between Laura and Gioconda is one of the most passionate in the repertory, the two women stalking the stage like two tigresses, fighting for the man they love! Gioconda, wild with jealousy, waves her dagger at Laura, only to melt into self-sacrifice when she sees her mother's rosary in the hands of her rival and realizes that it was Laura who saved her mother's life!

In the third act, Gioconda again appears from another of these mysterious hiding-places, this time in Alvise's palace, at the precise moment Laura is about to swallow the poison. The street-singer has brought Laura a sleeping potion as a substitute for the poison.

Many people feel that these highly contrived situations are too much even for such a flamboyant opera plot as that of "Gioconda." But modern rationalism of plot is hardly called for in a melodrama. It may be "sensational" for a husband to force an erring wife to take poison and then exhibit her corpse at a party, but, after all, any husband in love with his wife would be just as indignant at her faithlessness. He would endure the same torture, the same heartache, and very often the same strong desire for revenge. Nowadays he would simply express these feelings in a different fashion. The emotions are the same; it is only the methods that vary from century to century. The grand passions, the wicked deceits, the flesh and blood weaknesses, inherent in man and woman from the beginning of time, are underlined and underscored by Ponchielli and Boïto in words and music as telling as they are melodramatic!

Amilcare Ponchielli (1834-1886), teacher of Mascagni and Puccini, did not achieve success as an operatic composer until he was forty, when he revised an early opera, "I Promessi Sposi." Two years later he produced "La Gioconda," for which the composer Arrigo Boïto (1842-1918) had written a libretto, disguising his name under the anagram, Tobia Gorrio. The text was adapted from Victor Hugo's prose play, "Angelo, tyran de Padoue" (1835), the locale moved from Padua to Venice, the story from 1549 to the seventeenth century and without the political connotations; the mother of the heroine in the play is not blind but radical in her views and long since dead. Boïto also weakened the character of the second heroine, who, according to Hugo, was the rival of the street singer for the affections of both lover and husband!

The Hugo play, which inspired Mercadante and Eugène D'Albert, as well as Ponchielli, to write operas, is charged with the terrors of a tyrannized state, power politics, and government proscription. Although little of this theme remains in the opera, the violence is kept at fever heat by the music, while the realism anticipates the *verismo* of Ponchielli's pupils and successors.

The première at La Scala, Milan on April 8, 1876, was a triumphant success, due in part to the Spanish tenor, Giuliano Gayarré, who sang the role of Enzo. Maddalena Mariani-Masi, a Florentine soprano who had created the role of Boïto's Margarita in "Mefistofele", was the Gioconda, and Marietta Biancolini-Rodriguez, a famous interpreter of Bellini, sang Laura. The Barnaba, Gottardo Aldighieri, is also remembered as having written the words to Arditi's waltz, "The Kiss." Ormondo Maini was the Alvise and Barlani-Dini the Cieca.

"La Gioconda" was the first American première to be offered at the Metropolitan Opera House. The date was December 20, 1883, the conductor Auguste Vianesi. The cast was headed by Christine Nilsson, the Swedish soprano who sang Marguerite in "Faust" on the opening night, and who displayed "her strong tragic powers in an admirable light," according to Henry Krehbiel of the Tribune. Roberto Stagno's Enzo was criticized by the same reviewer for the lack of character in his delineation and "vicious traits" of vocalism. After only nine days of preparation, it is remarkable that Emmy Fursch-Madi as Laura, Sofia Scalchi as La Cieca, and Giuseppe Del Puente as Barnaba were all praised by Mr. Krehbiel for adding "to their representations as sterling artists." Only Franco Novara, as Alvise, owing to an indisposition, "did not reach the plane where his abilities usually move."

LOHENGRIN

"LOHENGRIN" is possibly the most popular of all of Wagner's operas. At the Metropolitan, it leads all the other Wagner works in number of performances, and stands third in the list of the most performed operas, directly after "Aïda" and "La Bohème." We may well ask what are the elements of "Lohengrin" that keep such a hold on the imagination and affections of so large a public. Of course, "Lohengrin" is one of the great love stories of literature. Also, at first glance, it might seem that "Lohengrin" is pretty much of a fairy story. The magic swan, the mysterious hero in shining armor who comes to rescue the maiden, the wicked witch Ortrud—these are all stock characters of fairy tale lore. But there is a great deal more to *Lohengrin*: it also happens to deal with some of the essential conflicts which rock the world today, the war between good and evil. In a sense Elsa and Ortrud represent two sides to human nature. Their music speaks clearly, now of Elsa, the pure maiden:

then of Ortrud, the temptress:

114

Lohengrin himself is, of course, symbolic of Wagner, the great artist, the great composer. His source of power is his musical genius. He dwells in the remote and brilliant realm of art and yet he yearns for human love, for the understanding heart of a woman. Lohengrin's tragedy is Wagner's. The hero, emerging from his godly realm, cannot share his source of inspiration with anyone. He cannot divulge his artistic creed and ideas to Elsa simply because she would not understand them. The opera enacts the tragedy of two human beings, the great artist who is doomed to solitude but who wants to be loved for his own sake as a human being, and a woman who, as a wife, quite rightfully wants to share all her husband's activities and experiences.

"Lohengrin" is also a religious opera. It is the story of divine and miraculous power come down from heaven to earth through a man consecrated to service. We hear a suggestion of this from the first notes of the Prelude. It has even been said that the divided strings suggest the shimmer of angels' wings:

At the end of the first act, all of Elsa's difficulties are seemingly over: her innocence is established, the man of her dreams is to be her husband. Her happiness seems assured; both literally and figuratively Lohengrin is the answer to a maiden's prayer. Why is it, then, that she loses him, that within a few hours all this promised happiness turns into tragedy?

One explanation of the change we find in the character of Ortrud. Wagner painted her in the darkest musical colors he could find. When the curtain opens in the second act we look

115

into the darkness of her soul and we listen to the orchestra paint Ortrud's wickedness. Ortrud is the negation of love. For her, all means justify the end, and the end is power. She is the symbol of tyranny. When she calls on the pagan gods in the second act even Telramund shudders. Her gods are the gods of evil, which seem to triumph. Ortrud sows her doubts in the heart of Elsa. The fatal question is asked and Lohengrin must reveal himself and return to the realm from which he came.

But evil does not triumph over the power of Lohengrin's faith, the power of good. He came in answer to Elsa's prayer in order to prove that she had not murdered her brother. It was her prayer, her faith, which brought Lohengrin to help her. And it is Lohengrin's prayer, the power of his faith, which restores Elsa's brother. Lohengrin was more than a man; he was a servant of the Holy Grail, in a sense a priest. He had the right to ask for faith, for only her faith made his presence possible.

Another factor underlies the profound message of "Lohengrin," the symbolism of the question itself. The forbidden question penetrates the literature of all lands, from the search of Orpheus for Eurydice to Adam's quest for the knowledge of good and evil.

"Lohengrin" is more than a fairy tale, more than a love story, more than a symbolic picture of an artist's life. It is primarily a message of faith which has won for the music drama a place among the greatest works of operatic literature for over a hundred years.

In spite of its celestial atmosphere of serenity, "Lohengrin" caused many headaches and heartaches to its composer, who was in Switzerland when he composed it.

Anyone with a drop of creative blood in his veins must feel for Wagner, who wrote: "I cannot allow my 'Lohengrin' to wither away unperformed." It might have done just that if it had not been for the generous intervention of Franz Liszt. This man was unique in his zeal for the work of others. No other composer devoted so much of his time and energies to furthering the careers of his colleagues. It is true that in 1850 Liszt had at his disposal the small opera house at Weimar, Germany, where he had settled down in the capacity of court musical director. So he was able to do something about it when Wagner addressed him in characteristically florid nineteenth century fashion: "Perform my 'Lohengrin!' You are the only one to whom I could address this prayer; to none but you should I entrust the creation of this opera; to you I give it with perfect and joyous confidence." His confidence, however, was not so perfect that he didn't feel it necessary to warn Liszt to avoid all cuts. "Give the opera as it is; cut nothing!"

Fortunately for us, all these negotiations and arrangements had to be transacted by letter, for Wagner was in political exile from Germany. The composer could not even attend the first performance of his beloved "Lohengrin." He thought of sneaking over the border and attending incognito, but Liszt vetoed this plan as too risky. The resultant advantage to us was that all his comments had to be entrusted to paper. We know a great deal more about this performance than if Wagner had been there.

Liszt seems to have done everything humanly possible to carry out all Wagner's intentions. He undertook all the rehearsals himself and was able to assure Wagner that "it is understood that we shall not cut a note, not an iota of your work, and that we shall give it in its absolute purity so far as it is in our power."

Wagner rebelled at the idea of sending metronome indications to Liszt; they were unnecessary . . . he had full reliance on Liszt's artistic sympathy, etc., etc. Then he sent a considerable list of precise timing indications! He put it very tactfully. "I send you these," he writes, "in confirmation, no doubt, of your own views."

It seemed as if Wagner would have things just the way he wanted them. And then the performance lasted one hour and fifteen minutes longer than he had counted on! Wagner was horrified and immediately inferred that the fault lay with the singers and their old-fashioned habits of reclaiming recitative sections very slowly. He writes an impassioned letter to Liszt urging him to call additional rehearsals, to make it clear to the performers that "Lohengrin" does not contain the usual type of recitative, that everything must be sung with great vitality and energy. The great blow came when, to his surprise, he learned from a friend who attended the performance, that the singers had sung everything, including the declamatory sections, up to tempo, just as Wagner desired. It seems the composer had simply miscalculated by an hour and a quarter! Sitting in his tiny Paris apartment, playing the score on the piano and singing it himself in his rather thin and weak voice, Wagner must have speeded things up unconsciously. He obviously failed to compensate for the very different conditions in the theater, for the opulent voices of the singers, and for the brilliant instrumental sonorities.

Wagner did not have an opportunity to hear any of the "Lohengrin" music until he conducted some excerpts from it at a concert in Switzerland some three years later. It is significant that even there he discovered that he had forgotten to notate one important change in tempo. The seven measures preceding the recapitulation of the "Wedding March" should be considerably slower.

"The impression must be one of solemn emotion or else the intention is lost."

If fate was not overly generous to Wagner at the time of the "Lohengrin" première, it certainly repaid him handsomely later. What other composer had at his disposal a model theater built according to his own specifications and an army of devoted and adoring assistants and performers who hung on his every word and vied in fulfilling his every desire?

The composer of words and music, Richard Wagner (1813-1883), was first inspired to write an opera on the theme of "Lohengrin" while living in poverty at 14 Rue Jacob, Paris, in the winter of 1841-42. A hopeless failure in the French capital, the composer was moved by nostalgic patriotism to an interest in early German history. He completed the sketch on August 3, 1845, when he took with him to Marienbad a copy of the anonymous epic as well as the Simrock edition of Wolfram

119

von Eschenbach's medieval poem, on which the libretto is based. Wagner sketched the music on a three-month holiday to Gross-Graupe, a village near Dresden, in the early summer of 1846, but did not finish the third act until March 5, 1847; the first act, June 8; the second, August 2 and the Prelude, August 28. The scoring was completed by March, 1848. Involved in the political agitations of Germany in 1848-49, Wagner was living as a proscribed exile in Switzerland when he persuaded his future father-in-law and devoted disciple, Franz Liszt, to present "Lohengrin" for the first time in Weimer. At the première (August 28, 1850) the orchestra was limited to thirty-eight men; four peasants acted as the *cortège* of the hero, there were no supers for the procession, and the scenery was a dilapidated assemblage of earlier settings.

The first Lohengrin was Carl Beck, a former pastry-cook of Weimar. His Elsa was Rosa Aegthe, whose husband, Theodor von Milde, sang the role of Telramund. Messrs. Hoefer and Paetsch appeared as King Henry and his herald, respectively, while Liszt, "all fire and flame" as Ernest Newman points out, took charge on the podium.

The American première of "Lohengrin" took place at the German Stadt Theater in New York on April 3, 1871, with Theodor Habelmann, later a Metropolitan stage director, in the title role. Louise Lichtmay was Elsa and Marie Frederici, who had created Marguerite in Philadelphia eight years before, was Ortrud. Messrs. Vierling and Franosch sang Telramund and King Henry. Wilhelm Formes was the Herald, and Adolf Neuendorff, who was to introduce "Die Walküre" to America six years later, conducted the performance with such success that it was repeated ten times within the month.

On the eighth subscription night of the Metropolitan's inaugural season, November 7, 1883, "Lohengrin" was first pre-

sented at the opera house, in Italian. Italo Campanini and
Christine Nilsson, who had impersonated Faust and Marguerite
on opening night the preceding week, sang the roles of Lohengrin and Elsa "to the best possible advantage" according to contemporary opera-goers. Emmy Fursch-Madi, another Marguerite
in her earlier days, was Ortrud; Giuseppe Kaschmann, first
Metropolitan Count di Luna, the Telramund. Franco Novara
was King Henry; and Ludovico Contini the Herald. Auguste
Vianesi, a naturalised Frenchman of Italian birth, conducted.

LUCIA DI LAMMERMOOR

A CERTAIN aura of mystery has always seemed to surround the art of musical composition, and perhaps it always will. But those who picture Donizetti, the composer of "Lucia," as retiring to an ivory tower and there, amid fasting and meditation, waiting for musical inspiration to descend on him like some bolt of psychic lightning from above, could not be further from the truth. On the contrary, confronted with a commission to write a new opera, Donizetti went to work with a brisk efficiency that would do credit to a twentieth-century business man. He proceeded straightway to his commodious filing cabinet, where neatly indexed under headings like arias, duets, trios, ensemble pieces, choral numbers, was every bit of unused musical material he had ever composed: things that had been cut out of earlier works, isolated numbers, brief ideas sketched but not yet fully developed, miscellaneous scraps from his notebooks, every sort of tonal item!

Donizetti was not the man to let even a stray sixteenth note go to waste! He reminds one of a thrifty housewife, putting down her surplus garden produce, market bargains, and left-overs in the deep freeze. But even making every allowance for his well-stocked freezer, we must admit that Donizetti was a whirlwind cook.

The story goes that one of his most successful operas, "The Elixir of Love," was commissioned only two weeks before the day of its performance.

That means that Donizetti and his librettist, Romani, had only two weeks in which to find a text and put it in libretto form. Then Donizetti had to compose and orchestrate the music, have the instrumental and vocal parts copied, rehearse the singers and the orchestra, and, finally, stage it.

One strongly suspects that the pleasures of the table were not unduly neglected during this period. Donizetti's enjoyment of food was well known to his friends. It seems that he was particularly fond of spaghetti, and the famous singer, the basso Lablache, was equally fond of preparing it to Donizetti's taste. On one occasion there was a gala spaghetti feast at Lablache's house, but Donizetti arrived late and the food was all gone. Lablache readily agreed to return to the kitchen and produce a new batch on the condition that Donizetti write a few bars of music in the album of one of the other guests, the Countess Merlini. Souvenir albums were quite the fashion in those days. It took Donizetti only twenty minutes to fill two pages of the album, by which time Lablache arrived to reward him with a steaming platter of his favorite dish. However, Donizetti sent out a hurried call two days later, asking to see the album again; in the meantime he had thought the matter over and decided to make use of the music he had composed in such a hurry. And so what had started out in life as a graceful little waltz in the Countess Merlini's album, became, in due time, the servants' chorus in "Don Pasquale."

Even though he never let a note go to waste, Donizetti's output must still be considered prodigious. Between 1824 and 1828 he composed no less than ten operas, a lifetime's work for most composers. During the same period he wrote various works in other forms, and he revised earlier operas and added new pieces to them.

For all his technical facility, Donizetti insisted, almost to the point of religious conviction, that the one overwhelmingly important ingredient of music is always a beautiful melody. He used to say: "If you want to find out if a certain piece of music is good, play the melody without the accompaniment."

By such a test his own music would pass triumphantly. His accompaniments are very simple. Indeed, the simplicity of Donizetti's musical background was a matter of principle with him; that is the way he *chose* to write. He certainly was not confined to that style by any technical limitations of his own. And yet, although melody was the very cornerstone of Donizetti's musical philosophy, the advice he gave to his own students suggests that the science of music was also important to him. "Write as many fugues and exercises as you can and orchestrate them diligently," he told his pupils. Another eminently practical but surprising idea, coming from Donizetti, is found in his statement: "I am very grateful to my teacher Bertolo that he made me study all the string quartets of Haydn, Beethoven and Mozart. Through this careful understanding of counterpoint, I learned how to spin out a musical composition at times even when I had very few ideas of real value."

Donizetti's point of view, placing melody before all else, has been vindicated by the enduring success of his works. His musical ideas were right for *him* at least. He wrote according to his own musical convictions, just as Wagner wrote according to his very different convictions.

That, perhaps, is something that *all* great composers have in common, even though their musical philosophies may be poles apart: fidelity to their own deep convictions. In other words, music which lives does so not because it has been written in this or that particular style, but because it has been written with passionate conviction, from the heart. It is inevitable that there be disagreement among composers. The wonderful variety of the operatic repertory is testimony to the variance of musical opinion that has existed among composers. It was a happy day for us all when composers agreed to disagree; let us hope they always will.

~~~~~~~~~~~~~

Gaetano Donizetti (1797-1848), drawn to a Scotch theme perhaps by his own ancestry (his grandfather, Donald Izett, is said to have been a weaver from Perthshire), wrote "Lucia" to a text which Salvatore Cammarano (1801-1852) had constructed on Sir Walter Scott's novel, "The Bride of Lammermoor" (1819). Other operas on the same plot had been composed by Bredal (1822), Carafa (1829), and Mazzucato (1834). Sir Walter founded his romance on an actual tragedy which took place in Scotland in 1669, when Janet Dalrymple attacked the bridegroom, David Dunbar, whom her father, Viscount Stair, had insisted that she marry rather than Dunbar's uncle, Lord Rutherfurd, to whom she was secretly betrothed. The account of this melodramatic event was not published in full until 1823, when the Rev. Andrew Symson exposed the facts. In 1827 a fuller account, embellished with supernatural agencies, was written by Charles Kirkpatrick Sharpe in his notes to Law's "Memorials."

Edgardo's final aria, "Tu che a dio spiegasti d'ali," was tossed off by the composer in half an hour while suffering from a severe headache, as he admitted to his wife while they were playing cards with some friends—Persico; Louis Gilbert Duprez, the first Edgardo; and Cosselli, the first Ashton. Donizetti designed the role of Lucia specifically for Fanny Tacchinardi-Persiani, the Roman coloratura who sang it at the première in the San Carlo Opera House in Naples on November 26, 1835. Other roles were taken by Giacchini (Arturo), Porto (Raimondo), Zappucci

(Alisa) and Rossi (Normanno). The exhilaration of the occasion was so intense that the delicate composer went to bed with a fever.

"Lucia de Lammermoor" reached the United States in a French production at the Théâtre d'Orléans in New Orleans on May 28, 1841. Auguste Nourrit, brother of the more famous Adolphe, was the Edgardo, and Julia Calvé (no kin of the great Carmen, Emma Calvé) sang the title role. The conductor was Eugène Prosper-Prévost.

"Lucia" was the second opera to be presented at the Metropolitan, serving also as a debut vehicle for young Sembrich on October 24, 1883, two nights after the opening "Faust." Praised by Mr. Henderson of the Times for her "faultless execution" and facility of expression," the soprano was also hailed by Mr. Krehbiel for her "exquisite style" and "thoroughly musical nature." The first Metropolitan Edgardo was Italo Campanini; the first Ashton, Giuseppe Kaschmann, who possessed "a handsome face and figure" and "considerable talent as an actor" but was afflicted by a tremolo which distressed the reviewer of the Tribune. Vincenzo Fornaris sang Arturo on this occasion; Amadeo Grazzi was the Normanno, and Imogene Forti the Alisa.

MADAMA BUTTERFLY

THE FIRST performance of "Madama Butterfly" took place on the 17th of February, 1904, at La Scala Opera House in Milan. The cast was an excellent one, the preparation had been painstaking. The composer had already proved himself a favorite with the public. And yet, the opera was a failure, one of the most complete fiascos in operatic history. Seldom has a work been so thoroughly rejected by both the audience and the press.

Have you ever wondered how a famous composer feels after witnessing a disastrous outcome of the first presentation of a new and cherished work? Then listen to the following account, in Puccini's own words, as recounted to us by his biographer, Arnaldo Fraccaroli. "It was a terrible evening. The failure of 'Butterfly' hurt me all the more because it was a complete surprise. I loved this work too much to believe the judgment of those who rejected it. Was it possible that all of us had been mistaken: I, the singers, Maestro Campanini, Giulio Ricordi, the orchestra players? I could see that all those who had been present at the rehearsals had been sincerely moved. They loved my little Japanese girl as much as I loved her. While writing the opera, I could see her in front of me, this little girl so sweet and melancholy. I followed her step by step, imagined her sitting on the hillock looking out at the sea, waiting . . . waiting . . . I was so certain that the opera would be well received that I invited my two sisters to witness the première, my sisters whom I had never before exposed to the uncertainties of a first performance; and there was my own family, my boy, Tonio, who was only fifteen. Poor dears, how deeply they were hurt by that unholy spectacle! At once, that very evening, I decided to withdraw the score. At the time, although I was hurt, I still had the courage to protest; but the next morning I was completely broken. It wasn't so much the futility of three years' labor that I was lamenting, but somehow all my hopes were gone, and there was the great sadness in the realization that the dream of poetry which I had cherished with so much love was destroyed and broken! The morning after I felt I would never be able to write another note of music. Throughout the day, newspaper boys kept passing underneath my windows near La Scala yelling the headlines: '*Il fiasco del maestro Puccini!*' For two weeks afterward I couldn't force myself to leave the house . . . I was so ashamed ! ! ! "

We can only guess today at the reasons for the audience's hostility on that ill-fated 17th of February. It has been suggested that the political atmosphere in connection with the Russo-Japanese war made a sympathetic presentation of the Japanese people unpopular. This may have been a contributing factor, but undoubtedly the more important reason was that the first night audience did not expect the opera either to look or to sound as it did. The unfamiliar style of the music puzzled the public; various little details of Japanese behavior struck the Italians as ridiculous. And just as soon as the unusual qualities of the work affected their risibilities rather than their emotions, the opera was doomed to failure.

Luckily, Giacomo Puccini could learn as much from disaster as he gleaned from success. He went back to the score with his blue pencil, and the revival at the Teatro Grande in Brescia in the spring of the same year was the first of a long series of triumphs. The operatic world quickly accepted the exotic nature of the story and learned to appreciate the musical juxtaposition of East and West which is the essence of the work.

For Puccini, the far East and the far West were equally irresistible. Japan, China, and California serve as backgrounds for "Madama Butterfly," "Turandot," and "The Girl of the Golden West," but it was the Japan of "Butterfly" which required the most careful study of authentic local color on the part of the composer. In "Turandot" and "The Girl of the Golden West," all the characters of the play belong to the same surroundings, while the basic idea of "Butterfly" required a sharp distinction between the natives and the foreigners. On the one hand we have the oriental world of Cio-Cio-San and Goro, Yamadori, and Suzuki and their chirruping chorus of companions. On the other we find the American, or shall we say the Italian, features of Pinkerton, his wife, and the kindly Sharpless. It was Puccini's function to develop that dramatic and musical contrast by endowing his characters with music which would seem, in one instance, to be typical of far eastern Japan; in the other of the western world.

To represent Japan, Puccini used not only authentic Japanese folk tunes but composed in addition a number of melodies that to western ears are indistinguishable from the genuine ones. The melody which we hear in the orchestra at the entrance of Cio-Cio-San is the most famous of all the *Nagauta* (long-song) melodies, sung by blind musicians in the district of Kyoto.

But it would be difficult to guess that Suzuki's invocation of her gods at the opening of the second act is an imitation:

To achieve this illusion of Japanese music, Puccini had recourse to the pentatonic, or five-tone scale, which forms the basis of many oriental melodies and which may easily be found on the piano by playing the black keys only.

It might be thought that this tonal limitation would produce a thin and monotonous effect. The results, on the contrary, are magnificent, rich, and full-bodied musically, as for instance in the tragic outburst of the heroine when she carries her little son for Sharpless to see:

To American ears, the music allotted to Pinkerton and Sharpless may seem to be less than ideally representative of the United States, but it does, of course, provide a complete contrast to the oriental pages of the score and sounds definitely western, if not necessarily American. The "Star-Spangled Banner," or at least its opening phrase, is used to good advantage. The very changes the composer makes in treating it are very instructive: he omits the first two notes but, to compensate for this, develops a subsidiary turn of the phrase which permits him to integrate the melody with the rest of the music and yet keep it recognizable and therefore symbolic of Lieutenant Pinkerton's homeland.

Most of the occidental music in "Madama Butterfly" is essentially Italian in style. The entire love duet at the close of the first act contains all the fervor, romance, and tunefulness of Italian opera. But then, as the curtain falls, we return to the typical pentatonic melody of Japan:

131

In the play which David Belasco had fashioned from the story of John Luther Long, Puccini found ideal material for his operatic treatment. Today we can only marvel that the first reaction to this exciting work should have been so thoroughly negative. First impressions are not always to be trusted!

Giacomo Puccini wrote the score of "Madama Butterfly" in 1902, two years after he had attended a London performance of the play which David Belasco (1855-1931) had written on John Luther Long's story in Century Magazine. The novelette was founded on a tale brought back from Nagasaki by Mrs. Irvin Henry Correll, wife of a Methodist missionary and sister of Mr. Long. The prototype of Cio-Cio-San has been variously identified with Tsuru Yamamura, a young geisha of the city and also with the daughter of a sumarai, Date.

Puccini, who was in London to witness "Tosca," was deeply

impressed by the one-act play, to which he had been invited by Frank Neilson, the stage manager of Covent Garden.

The librettists, Luigi Illica (1857-1919) and Giuseppe Giacosa (1847-1906), followed the original scheme of a single act but divided it into two scenes. After an unsuccessful première at La Scala, the composer altered the opera by further dividing it into what are actually three acts and adding a final aria for Pinkerton ("Addio, fiorito asil!"). In this form it achieved the first hint of its lasting success in Brescia on May 28, 1904.

At the première in Milan, February 17, 1904, Rosina Storchio sang the title role which Blanche Bates had created in Belasco's play (Herald Square Theater, New York, March 5, 1900). "So true, so fine, so moving is your wonderful art," the composer wrote her. Giovanni Zenatello was the Pinkerton, and Giuseppe de Luca the Sharpless, twelve years before his Metropolitan debut. Gaetano Pini-Corsi sang Goro; Venturini was the Uncle Priest, and P. Wulmann the Yakuside, a role later omitted. Giuseppina Giaconia was the Suzuki. Cleofonte Campanini, younger brother of the renowned tenor, conducted.

"Madama Butterfly" first reached the United States on October 15, 1906, presented in English by the Henry W. Savage Company at the Columbia Theater in Washington, D.C. Elsa Szamosy, a young Hungarian soprano and former child piano prodigy, made her debut as Cio-Cio-San, alternating with Florence Easton; Harriet Behnee was the Suzuki. Renée Vivienne, later promoted to the title role, was Kate Pinkerton. Joseph Sheehan, who organized his own company some time later, sang Pinkerton, while Winfred Goff was Sharpless. Walter Rothwepp conducted.

Four months later, on February 11, 1907, "Madama Butterfly" was introduced to the Metropolitan stage with Geraldine Farrar singing the first of her ninety-five performances of the leading

133

role in this theater. Enrico Caruso and Antonio Scotti brought to the roles of Pinkerton and Sharpless an expertness derived from earlier performances in London. Louise Homer was Suzuki, and Helen Mapleson, wife of the Metropolitan's librarian, the Kate. Albert Reiss was Goro; Giovanni Paroli, Yamadori; Adolf Mühlmann, the Uncle-Priest; Arcangelo Rossi, the Commissary. Arturo Vigna, who had come to New York with Caruso, conducted.

"Through every measure of the performance . . . was to be perceived the fine Italian hand of Mr. Puccini himself," wrote the Times critic, Richard Aldrich, who noted the "delicacy, the shifting beauty, and the completely penetrating atmosphere" of the production.

THE MAGIC FLUTE

FOR Christoph Willibald Gluck, the first concern in writing an opera was not musical beauty but rather the psychological truth of the drama enacted on the stage. Sometimes, according to the composer's own confession, he was impelled to compose sounds that hesitated, sounds that indicated excitement, in order to express the hesitation and excitement of his characters. For him the all-important concern was to write music which was "true to Nature" and to make the audience believe in the reality projected before them.

Mozart, on the other hand, is on record as placing music ahead of all other considerations. And yet Mozart, like Gluck, used his musical inspiration to bring out the full extent of the poetic idea. "The orchestra must live the same imaginary life as the singer," he said, admitting that certain of his operatic sequences would not have been justified in symphonic music but are indispensable in depicting contrasts or conflicts of character.

It is especially appropriate to find such stress of musical truthfulness in "The Magic Flute," which is, actually, a story of man's spiritual growth, his progress toward wisdom and light.

All through the score we find traces of Mozart's unflinching pursuit of an exact and inspired verisimilitude reflecting his characters and circumstances in musical terms.

Two of his characters, Pamina and Papageno, for example, attempt suicide during the course of the opera. These two episodes have so much in common that the composer uses the

135

same key and even the same succession of chords in depicting them. Yet for Pamina the situation is a deadly serious one:

For Papageno, on the other hand, it is a case of sheer pretense:

Another delicate bit of musical perceptiveness is disclosed during Tamino's aria, addressed to the portrait of Pamina. Both orchestra and singer become breathless, inflamed with passion for the beautiful girl. The orchestra seems almost human. The singer cannot help but be carried away. He looks at Pamina's picture, and says, "Oh, if she were only standing before me. If I could only find her! Why, I would . . . I would . . . "

At this point there is a long silence. Tamino concentrates on the picture. Then and only then does he realize that if Pamina were standing there beside him, he would embrace her, press her to his heart, and call her his forever.

Equally sensitive is the musical usage during the scene in which Tamino comes to the three temples. Refused admittance at the temples of Reason and Nature, he finally knocks at the gates of Wisdom.

The priest emerges and listens patiently to Tamino's attack

137

on Sarastro before he tells the young prince that it is Sarastro who rules the place.

"So all these temples and all this beauty are sham and hypocrisy," exclaims the impatient youth. As long as Tamino is certain of Sarastro's guilt, the music moves definitely in the key of F minor.

Just as he is at the point of leaving, however, and completing his cadence, the priest steps in to show him that his thoughts are false. The music is suddenly and harshly interrupted by an unprepared C minor sequence.

This moment is of the greatest importance. Tamino, who was convinced that Sarastro is a villain, is shown to be wrong. He was certain of his F minor convictions; now he is shown that he was wrong; the truth is in C minor.

Many of us grow up believing that certain things are evil and eventually wake up to realize that our convictions are founded on flimsy ground. Life in itself is a process of revealing and maturing experiences, which Mozart symbolized in the simple terms of a fairy story.

Perhaps the most striking moment in the opera is another variation of this theme, the dramatic chorale sung by the armed men in the third act. The string choir of the orchestra conveys a mood of sheer despair, weeping, complaining, toiling, representing, as it were, the sorrows of humanity.

Above them, in calm and majestic tones, the armed men sing the chorale, "Oh Lord in heaven, look down upon us," proclaiming that if man can be steadfast, endure tribulations, and overcome the fear of death itself in his search for truth, he will be free.

Where the fear of death is mentioned, a heart-rending discord seems to cut the ear like a knife:

And then, as soon as the chorale is finished, Tamino uttters the sentence which seems to many the most beautiful in the whole opera, and which expresses so eloquently the central theme of this work:

After the ancient chorale, more than two centuries old, only the music of Mozart could lift men's hearts still higher and bring this lofty scene to a fitting conclusion.

140

᠁᠁᠁᠁᠁᠁᠁

The official librettist, impresario and first comedian of "The Magic Flute" was Emanuel Schikaneder (1748-1812), who commissioned the fairy-opera for his suburban playhouse, the Theater auf der Wieden. The plot was taken from a pseudo-oriental tale, "Lulu, or the Magic Flute," in a collection published by Wieland in 1789 under the title "Dschinnistan." In order not to duplicate another opera launched by Schikaneder's rival, Marinelli, at another Vienna theater under the title of "Kaspar der Fagottist," certain modifications were made to the libretto of "The Magic Flute" while it was still in progress. These were reputedly accomplished by a prominent Freemason, Ignaz von Born, and by Johann George Metzler, a versatile lawyer, mineralogist and tenor who sang in the first cast of "The Flute" under the name of Carl Ludwig Giesccke. Masonic rituals were interpolated from "Sethos," a book by the French abbé, Jean Terrasson.

From May to July, 1791, Mozart toiled at the score, hard-pressed by poverty, ill-health, and even hunger, his wife ill in Baden, where she entertained herself with a sympathetic officer. The wily Schikaneder installed the composer in a little garden house in the courtyard of his theater. In the late summer and early autumn the new opera was orchestrated, the first performance taking place at the Theater auf der Wieden on September 30, 1791, Mozart himself conducting from the clavier, barely two months before his death.

Schikaneder, the impresario, was the first Papageno, with Nannina Gottlieb as Pamina. In a letter dated October 7-8, 1791, Mozart describes with pleasure how the baritone-soprano duet was repeated by these artists at the request of the public. The

141

first Queen of the Night was Josefa Weber, Mozart's sister-in-law, who had married the Court violinist, Franz Hofer. The Papagena was Mme. Gerl, with whom the composer enjoyed a brief flirtation and whose husband sang the role of Sarastro. Benjamin Schack found his own skill as a flautist convenient in the part of Tamino. His wife enacted the Third Lady in the group led by Mmes. Klopfer and Hoffmann. Nonseul was Monostatos. The Speaker was Herr Winter; the three priests were an elder Schikaneder and Messrs. Kistler and Moll, while the three slaves comprised Messrs. Giesecke, Frasel and Stark.

An English version of "The Magic Flute" by Charles E. Horn, who himself sang Sarastro, was used for its New York première on April 17, 1833. The performance took place at the Park Theater and was followed by a farce, "Everybody's Husband." The cast included Mrs. Henry Wallack, earlier known as the beautiful Miss Turpin of Liverpool, who sang the Queen of the Night; John Jones as Tamino; Miss Sharpe as Papagena and Miss Austin as Pamina. Henry Placide was the Papageno; John Fisher, Monostatos; and Mr. Hayden, the Speaker. Some authorities cite an earlier production on March 7, 1832, in Philadelphia.

A fabulous cast was assembled by Maurice Grau for the Metropolitan première of "The Magic Flute," which took place in Italian as "Il Flauto Magico." Marcella Sembrich "was unable to do herself justice as the Queen," wrote Mr. Henderson in the Times. Andreas Dippel "was a respectable Tamino," Giuseppe Campanari "gave a good Papageno, and Pol Plançon a grave and sonorous Sarastro." Emma Eames "was a lovely picture and sang her music well" as Pamina. The rest of the cast comprised Zélie de Lussan as Papagena; Milka Ternina, Eugenia Mantelli, and Carrie Bridewell as the Three Ladies; Suzanne Adams, Eleanor Broadfoot, and Rosa Olitzka as the

Three Youths; Antonio Pini-Corsi as Monostatos; Eugène Dufriche as the Speaker. Messrs. Adolf Mühlmann and Roberto Vanni were the two priests; Messrs. Meux and Maestri, the Guards. Luigi Mancinelli conducted, and the production was outstanding for its "gorgeous scenes" and "the splendor of its scenic attire," according to the Times.

MANON

ONE DAY J. Massenet was taking a long walk through the streets of Paris. The composer's Christian name, known to biographers as Jules but quoted by himself as Julien is, indicated by an initial for a good reason. Massenet had a peculiar aversion to his first name and never permitted it to be spelled out in any announcements or publications. Out of respect for an innocent phobia of a distinguished musician, we shall do likewise. On the occasion of this particular walk, his mind was full of the new opera which he had already started to compose on the basis of Abbé Prévost's novel "Manon Lescaut."

Suddenly the composer happened to notice a young girl, a florist's assistant, delicate, fragile, yet abundantly full of life. In her dancing eyes he seemed to detect a longing for luxury and pleasure. "There she is," he said to himself. "That is Manon!" And all during the composition of the opera, the remembered image of this girl, whom he had seen only a moment and had never spoken to, was constantly before him.

This reliance on visual inspiration was typical of Massenet. The testimony of his friends and many hints in his memoirs make it clear that he was, if we may be permitted to use such a word, a "visualist." In orchestrating his opera "The King of Lahore," for instance, he is said to have kept a little enameled oriental box on his desk; its deep blue speckled with gold guided him, supposedly, in the selection of the exotic colors for his instrumentation.

Such a gift is, of course, invaluable to a man of the theater.

Massenet literally saw the characters of his operas move, gesticu-
late, and act right in front of his inner eye. It is no wonder
that his music evokes them in such startling physical detail.

Consider the contrast in the musical presentation of the two
principal men in the story, des Grieux and Lescaut.

The orchestra tells us quite plainly that Lescaut is a soldier, a
hail-fellow-well-met, a vigorous, unscrupulous, rather dashing
character:

Des Grieux, on the other hand, is a gentle, romantic figure:

But the personage Massenet painted with especial care was,
of course, that "astonishing sphinx and veritable siren," Manon
herself.

With infinite care Massenet spied on her every movement
and facial expression, reproducing it in music supple, subtle, and
true to life.

In the very first scene, we see the little girl on her way to
convent school, inexperienced in the ways of the world, a little
timid in the presence of such a throng of people. Her steps are

145

hesitant, as if she were feeling her way in her strange surroundings:

But Manon is not merely shy. She is thrilled by the first trip
that she has made alone and by her first glimpse into the world
which she finds so glamorous. She bubbles with enthusiasm,
apologizing to her cousin, Lescaut, for her excitement and
pointing out that, after all, this is her first trip:

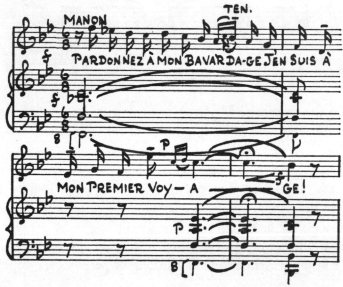

She may be just a sweet innocent girl from the country, but the blood of the pleasure-loving Lescauts courses through her veins, and she makes us realize how hungry she is for the enjoyments she has never known as a girl. "Oh, how I should like to have fun like this all my life," she exclaims:

For a moment she abandons the wild dreams, the yearning for glamor and adventure which have been excited by a glimpse of the three gay Parisian beauties, Poussette, Javotte, and Rosette. Reflecting on the monotonous life that awaits her in school, she sings a sad little mazurka:

147

Manon's vacillating nature is the clue to all the tragedy that follows. In the second act she voices her affection for her first lover, des Grieux. Only a few minutes later she sighs and dreams of the riches and luxury that will be hers if she gives in to the wealthy Brétigny.

In the third act she is a brilliant courtesan, reveling. in her glory as the best-dressed and most bejewelled woman in all Paris. Even her music preens itself as she accepts the homage of the Cours-la-Reine:

There is something touchingly honest about Manon's passion for luxury. When she dies, she seems tragically resigned to her fate. Even at the point of death, something of the young, coquettish Manon reasserts itself. She catches a sight of the evening star, but to her it suggests only a flashing diamond.

Massenet's desire to convert visual impressions into their musical counterparts required a new and special technique of composition, and he succeeded in developing an astonishing facility for inflecting a melodic line and making it flow forth as naturally and spontaneously as human speech itself. The hearer does not get the impression of any strict musical rhythm superimposed on the words but rather of the changing and varied rhythms of natural speech. We hear our heroine, instead of following an arbitrary four-four or three-four beat, rushing along in her excitement, sometimes breaking off altogether, sometimes slowing down as if searching for the next words:

This knack of writing a vocal line that seems absolutely spontaneous is one of Massenet's greatest virtues as a composer and, incidentally, his most important contribution to the musical theater.

All this is familiar territory to the present-day opera lover. We are apt to take it for granted, or what is a little sad, we hardly notice it at all. When Massenet began his career all this was new and not a little bewildering. Singers and conductors were used to strict successions of beats and meters, sounds encased in a comfortable corset of even pulses. In his memoirs, Massenet tells us how necessary his own presence was at first wherever his operas were performed; how he had to travel from city to city explaining, guiding, and clarifying his intentions to conductors, stage-directors, and singers. He accomplished his task admirably, people quickly became familiar with his style, and his works achieved world-wide success. The next two gen-

149

erations, with their usual contempt for the favorite art of their parents and grandparents, shrugged Massenet off as a sugary sentimentalist of little consequence. But esthetic judgments keep adjusting themselves, and the Massenet stock is again becoming a good investment. That "adorable" Manon which saw the light of day on the 19th of January, 1884, carries the imprint of genius that has long survived the seductive smile of the little Paris flower girl.

J. Massenet (1842-1912) was not the first to write operatic music for the "History of the Chevalier des Grieux and Manon Lescaut," famous tale of the Abbé Antoine Francois Prévost d'Exile (1697-1763). Halévy's ballet-pantomime had appeared in 1830; six years later Balfe produced a new stage version. Barrière and Fournier led Manon to the stage in 1851, and Auber did so in 1856.

The origin of the Massenet opera is uncertain. One version has it that the composer found the Prévost book on a shelf in the library of his librettist, Henri Meilhac, in the autumn of 1881. Another story says that Massenet started on the score in the summer of 1881 and worked at it several months the following year, first in the Abbé's own house at the Hague and later in Brussels. In the autumn of 1882 he asked the librettists, Meilhac and his colleague Philippe Gille (1831-1901), to an initial hearing. He also invited Léon Carvalho, general manager of the Opéra-Comique, and his wife, the former Caroline Miolan, to whom the work is dedicated.

By the Spring of 1883 "Manon" was completed, its orchestration neatly indicated in Massenet's unfaltering autograph. Since

Mme. Carvalho was unable to interpret the title role, it was given to Marie Heilbronn at the première, which took place on January 19, 1884, at the Opéra-Comique in Paris under the baton of Jean Daubé. On this occasion Alessandro Talazac sang des Grieux; Emil Alexandre Taskin was Lescaut; and Cobalet the Count des Grieux. Mmes. Molé-Triffier, Chevalier, and Rémy were Poussette, Javotte, and Rosette, while the Messrs. Grivot and Collin impersonated Guillot and Brétigny. The role of the maid was created in the second act for Blanche Arral, who in later life, as Mrs. George Wheeler, the wife of a New Jersey educator, reported that Massenet changed the part from a lackey to a maid in order to give her a place in the première.

When "Manon" was first presented in the United States, Massenet was not tagged "Mademoiselle Wagner," as he had been in Paris. The American première at the Academy of Music on December 23, 1885, offered in Italian, reminded the Herald reviewer of Mozart, Thomas, Gounod, and Bizet, but the Post found "no numbers which irresistibly captivate the mind." The Herald reported that Minnie Hauk acted the title role "with grace, piquancy and strong intelligence," although her tones were often "harsh and unmusical." The critics differed on the interpretation of des Grieux, which was sung by Francesco Giannini, the father of Dusolina and Vittorio. Lablache was considered in her element as Javotte. Her associates, Bauermeister and de Vigne, sang Poussette and Rosette. Cherubini "looked and acted like Papa Germont" as the Count; Foscanini drew little attention as Brétigny. Giuseppe Del Puente was the Lescaut and Rinaldini the Guillot under the Arditi baton.

"Manon" waited until January 16, 1895, to be heard at the Metropolitan and in its original French tongue, when Bauermeister and de Vigne repeated their roles of a decade before, joined by Marie Van Cauteren as Javotte. Massenet's beloved so-

151

prano, Sybil Sanderson, sang Manon, her voice described by Mr. Krehbiel as pure and true in intonation but "lacking in volume and penetrative quality." The impassioned singing of Jean de Reszke as des Grieux elicited the applause of a distinguished audience. Pol Plançon sang the Count, Armand Castelmary was Guillot and Victor Gromzeski was responsible for Brétigny, under the leadership of Emilio Bevignani.

Aïda, Act I, Scene 1. Hall in the palace at Memphis

Aïda, Act II, Scene 1. Amneris' apartments

Aïda, Act II, Scene 2.
A public square
in Thebes
Metropolitan Opera
Production: 1951-1952
Decor and costumes by
Rolf Gérard;
staging by
Margaret Webster

La Bohème, Act I. A garret. Metropolitan Opera Production: 1952-1953
Decor and costumes by Rolf Gérard; staging by Joseph L. Mankiewicz

La Bohème, Act III. A toll-gate at the edge of Paris

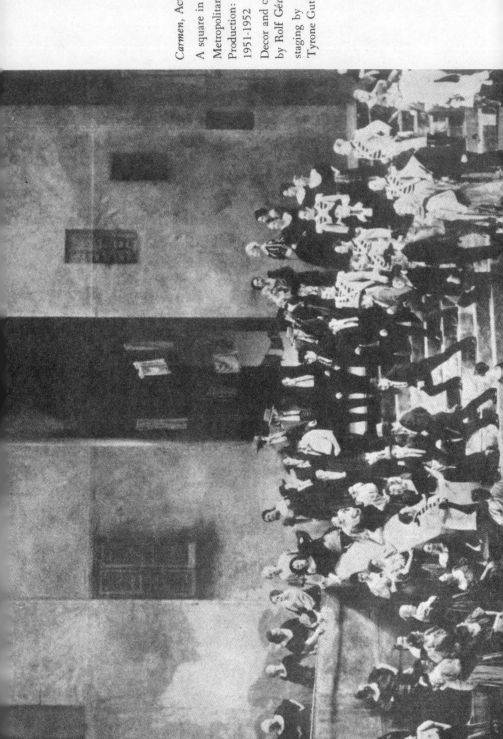

Carmen, Act I.
A square in Seville
Metropolitan Opera
Production:
1951-1952
Decor and costumes
by Rolf Gérard;
staging by
Tyrone Guthrie

Carmen, Act III. A mountain pass
Carmen, Act IV. Escamillo's quarters.

Cavalleria Rusticana.

A village in Sicily
Metropolitan Opera
Production: 1950-1951

Settings by
Horace Armistead;
costumes by
John Robert Lloyd;
staging by
Hans Busch

Cosi fan tutte, Act I, Scene 2. A garden by the sea
Metropolitan Opera Production: 1951-1952
Decor and costumes by Rolf Gérard; staging by Alfred Lunt

Cosi fan tutte, Act I, Scene 4. Another part of the garden

Don Carlo, Act I, Scene 2. Cloister gardens of the monastery of St. Just

Don Carlo,
Act II, Scene 2.
A square before
the cathedral

Don Carlo, Act III, Scene 1. The King's closet in Madrid
Metropolitan Opera Production: 1950-1951
Decor and costumes by Rolf Gérard;
staging by Margaret Webster

Don Carlo, Act IV.
Cloister of the monastery of St. Just

La Forza del Destino,
Act I, Scene 1.
Palace of the Marquis
of Calatrava
Metropolitan Opera
Production: 1952-1953
Decor and costumes by
Eugene Berman;
staging by Herbert Graf

La Forza del Destino, Act II. Italy, near a battlefield

La Forza del Destino, Act III, Scene 1.
The Cloister of Madonna degli Angeli

Lohengrin, Act II.
The castle courtyard
Metropolitan Opera
Production: 1952-1953
Decor redesigned by
Charles Elson;
staging by Dino Yannopoulos

Lohengrin, Act I.
Banks of the river Scheldt

Lohengrin, Act III, Scene 1.
Elsa's bridal chamber

Pagliacci, Act I

Metropolitan Opera
Production:
1950-1951

Settings by
Horace Armistead;

costumes by
John Robert Lloyd;

staging by
Max Leavitt

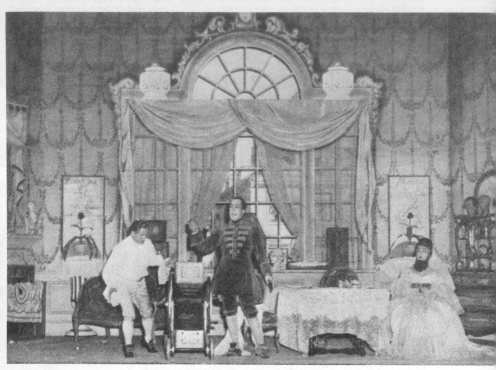

The Rake's Progress, Act II, Scene 3. Rakewell's morning room
Metropolitan Opera Production: 1952-1953
Decor and costumes by Horace Armistead;
staging by George Balanchine

The Rake's Progress, Act III, Scene 1. Rakewell's morning room

Rigoletto, Act I. The Duke's palace in Mantua

Rigoletto, Act II. Rigoletto's home
Metropolitan Opera Production: 1951-1952
Decor and costumes by Eugene Berman;
staging by Herbert Graf

Rigoletto, Act III. A room in the Duke's palace

THE MARRIAGE OF FIGARO

WHILE listening to Mozart's music, one is tempted to let the mind wander across four thousand miles of space and nearly two hundred years of time, back to the first of May, 1786, when Mozart's "Marriage of Figaro" had its first performance at the Imperial Court Theater in Vienna.

Mozart had prepared the performance himself; he had selected the cast, coached the singers, supervised the staging down to the last detail; finally he himself conducted the performance.

At this point one cannot help asking: how close are we today to the type of performance Mozart himself put into effect? How much of the genuine Mozart style have we been able to preserve? What do we know about his intentions? How authentic are our present day performances of this eighteenth-century masterpiece?

For one thing, stage lighting has been completely revolutionized since Mozart's day. On the modern stage, lights of all colors, shades, and intensities are available, and the men who operate them are guided by a number of detailed and complicated light cues. In Mozart's day, illumination was limited to oil lamps and candles, equipment lacking the power and flexibility of our present day, complicated switchboards. The stage looked quite different from ours, and these primitive lights had a definite influence on the style of the production.

In order to be visible, the singers of the eighteenth century had to play most of the time on the apron of the stage, close to the footlights. Further up-stage, details of facial expression, cos-

153

tume and behavior must have been rather difficult to perceive. As a result, eighteenth-century producers could attempt certain short-cuts which it would not be advisable to imitate on our well-lit stages. On the program of the Vienna première, for instance, Francesco Bussani is listed as singing both Bartolo, Figaro's long-missing father, and the troublesome gardener, Antonio. Yet there is only about a minute and a half available between Antonio's exit during the second act finale and Bartolo's entrance in all his pompous glory. Such a doubling of roles would hardly be feasible today. We have become accustomed to characteristic make-up, wigs, and costumes. In Mozart's day, apparently the outward appearance of certain characters was handled less carefully.

The lack of good visibility must have been a serious disadvantage in "The Marriage of Figaro," where the scenery and properties play such an important part in the action. The page-boy jumps out a window; people hide behind chairs, curtains and bushes, inside closets and garden houses. Unless clearly visible, these activities lose much of their impact.

Because of the lighting problems and the general stage conventions prevalent at the time, operatic acting was quite static in the eighteenth century. There was little movement or life on stage. It is apparent, however, from Mozart's letters, from reports of his contemporaries, and especially from the indications in his scores that he favored lively, realistic behavior on stage. The score of "The Marriage of Figaro" contains many clues to that effect.

In the hide-and-seek scene of the last act, for example, the Countess makes Cherubino believe that she is Susanna, while later Susanna appears to Figaro as the Countess. Mozart is not satisfied that the two women should merely exchange their hats and cloaks. He adds a musical disguise to the comedy. Both singers are directed to sing *con voce celata*—with disguised voice. As a matter of fact, both ladies succeed in their deception. When Figaro finally recognizes Susanna, it is only because at a certain point she forgets to change her voice. All this is clearly indicated in the score.

A contemporary witness reinforces our thesis still further. Among the Mandinis, Bussanis, and Benuccis, the Italian artists who sang in the first production of the opera under Mozart's direction, there was also a man whose name, in spite of its Italian spelling, sounds strange in such company: Michele Ochelli. This Michael O'Kelly was an Irishman who joined the Imperial Opera Company in Vienna, and, fortunately, not only sang tenor but also published memoirs. In the original production of "Figaro" O'Kelly played two parts: Basilio, the scheming music master, and Don Curzio, the stuttering judge. O'Kelly relates how he obtained Mozart's permission to stutter the part of Don Curzio not only during the recitative but also in the sextet itself, where his lines have to be coordinated to a fraction of a second with the singing of the five other performers and with the orchestra. Such stuttering could easily delay articulation and upset the rhythmical accuracy of a complicated musical ensemble. Mozart had his misgivings at first, but O'Kelly was obviously able to cope with the realistic stunt and still meet the demands of musical timing. He probably attacked the consonant ahead of time, so that by the time he sang the vowel he was exactly at the right spot. Mozart seemed to have been delighted with the idea once the correct execution was assured.

Mozart's concern with musico-dramatic niceties foreshadows methods used nowadays by our most progressive stage directors in the same way that his approach to the form of operatic composition laid the basis for nineteenth-century music drama.

We frequently hear a work of art spoken of as having been

155

"ahead of its time." That usually means that at first the work in question was thought to be obscure, difficult to grasp, and that many years had to pass before it finally found its audience. Mozart's "Marriage of Figaro" had no such history: it was a great success from the start and at its very first production was received enthusiastically by the public, as it has been ever since. And yet, I can think of no work to which the phrase "ahead of its time" can be more justly applied. It is, in fact, difficult to believe that such a monumental sequence as the great second-act finale was written over a century and a half ago. No one before Mozart had attempted such a long, uninterrupted piece of operatic music: about 150 pages in the full orchestral score. Composers of the eighteenth century wrote short numbers, each with a beginning and an end, strung together only by recitatives or by spoken dialogues. This finale foreshadows the whole trend of operatic development which took place in the nineteenth century, and reached its peak with Wagner, who finally did away completely with separate musical numbers and substituted instead an unbroken musical line!

In this "Figaro" finale there are seven musical numbers artfully welded together into one. This is continuous music drama written thirty-seven years before Wagner was born! Of course, Mozart was exceptionally lucky in two respects: he had at hand the masterly theatrical conception of the Beaumarchais play; he also had at his disposal the services of a highly skilled and experienced technician in the person of his librettist, Lorenzo da Ponte.

This second-act finale is so complicated that it is well to recall the situation involved and follow the detailed workings of the ingenious story step by step to the end of the act.

As part of Figaro's plan to embarrass the Count, the page-boy, Cherubino, is to masquerade as Susanna and keep a rendezvous

156

with the Count. Accordingly, Cherubino is brought to the Countess' room to try on Susanna's clothes. But suddenly the Count himself arrives and pounds impatiently on the door, forcing the half-dressed Cherubino to hide in the adjacent dressing room, actually an oversized closet. The Count has received an anonymous note in which the Countess is accused of planning a rendezvous with a lover. The locked closet door confirms the Count's suspicions, and he goes in search of a crowbar, taking his wife with him as a precaution against trickery. Now Susanna, who unbeknownst to the Count and the Countess was hiding behind a curtain, urges Cherubino to come out of the closet, and the page-boy, finding that his only means of escape is by way of the window, leaps out into the garden while Susanna promptly takes his place in the closet.

The Count and the Countess return, crowbar and all. Unaware of the substitution, and believing Cherubino to be in the closet, the Countess has no choice but to confess to the Count, who flies into a towering rage and demands that Cherubino come out at once. It is at this point that this unprecedented finale begins.

The Countess begs her husband to be lenient, particularly since Cherubino's appearance might seem to confirm his worst suspicions. The youth is in shirtsleeves and without a collar; he'd been trying on Susanna's dress.

This is too much for the Count. He loses his temper completely: "Give me the key," he shouts, and declares he will have vengeance. With drawn sword he approaches the ill-fated closet, but at this very moment its door opens, and to the Count's astonishment, as well as to the Countess' stupefaction, it is the maid who steps out!

"Susanna!" they cry out in turn:

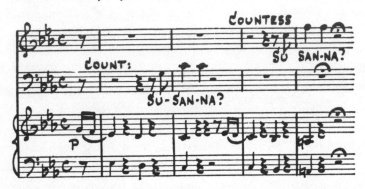

Notice how, without a break, we move smoothly into the next musical section. Within the space of two or three measures Mozart brings about a complete change of the emotional and musical climate.

The Count and the Countess are completely dumbfounded, while Susanna enjoys to the utmost the effect she is creating.

The Count decides to inspect the closet himself. This gives Susanna a chance to whisper to the Countess that Cherubino has made a successful escape. We have thus arrived at the third section of the finale where Mozart makes his first use of the flutes in the orchestra: a careful husbanding of his instrumental resources which allows him to build progressively from climax to climax.

The tables are turned on the Count, and the ladies press their advantage relentlessly: "It's only what you deserve," they sing.

158

There is still the little matter of the anonymous letter to be explained away, but since their plot has miscarried, the women confess to the Count that the letter was a hoax, written by Figaro. A general reconciliation follows, but at this moment we hear a knock announcing Figaro's entrance. Again the music proceeds directly on its way, stepping boldly into the key of G major from the previous key of B flat major. In this, the fourth section of the finale, Figaro invites the Count and Countess to come to the wedding festivity, and describes the joyful procession that is approaching:

We can observe at this point another example of that orchestral economy that we noticed a moment ago. "The trumpets are sounding," Figaro sings.

But they are not trumpets in the orchestra; they are oboes. If Mozart had had the resources of the large modern orchestra, he might not have had to be so cautious, but as it is, he is saving the trumpets for an important task later on. Now that Figaro is

159

on the scene, the Count has an opportunity to cross-examine him about the letter. But Figaro flatly denies the charge.

The women try to make Figaro confess that he wrote the letter, but he won't take the hint and continues to deny all knowledge of it. Everyone presses the Count to relent and give his consent to the marriage of Figaro and Susanna. His lordship is cornered and is saved from giving his reluctant go-ahead only by a knock on the door, which introduces section five.

Incidentally, every time people enter by the main door, their knocking is illustrated in the orchestra. The orchestral knocks are always different, yet unmistakeable. This time it is the tipsy gardener, Antonio, who is knocking.

He declares that he has seen a man jump out of the window. Just when everything was explained away, Antonio upsets it all again. Fortunately, Figaro is quick-witted enough to step into the breach and announce that it was he, Figaro, who jumped from the window.

The situation seems to be saved again. Figaro improvises quickly and describes the circumstances of his leap, even pretending that he has sprained his ankle during the fall.

E STRA-VOL TO M'HOUN NERVO DEL PIE.

And this leads us, as always without a break, into section six. Now comes a new problem. Antonio has found a piece of paper which Cherubino dropped in his flight. The Count seizes it, and asks Figaro what it is. Of course, Figaro doesn't know! "Now let's see . . . yes, of course . . . what was it again? It just slipped my mind for the moment." He is very pompous about it all, and stalls for time as best he can, until the women manage to help him out.

The Countess, peering over her husband's shoulder, recognizes the paper, and whispers to Susanna, who relates it to Figaro. He then makes his answer to the Count: "The paper is Cherubino's officer's commission . . . the boy left it with me because it was not properly sealed."

The Count has to be satisfied with the "explanation," and apparently nothing can now stand in the way of the marriage except—*another* knock on the door! Now, for the first time in the second act, both trumpets and kettle-drums are used, saved for this final climax!

Marcellina, supported by Bartolo and Basilio, vents her griev-
ance against Figaro. He has borrowed a substantial sum of
money from her and has promised either to repay it or to marry
her. Amid claims and denials, depositions and arguments, the
music proceeds with ever-mounting excitement until this grandiose finale comes to an end in the blaze of a magnificent *pres-
tissimo!*

We have moved without a break in the musical and dramatic
development from the Count's angry threat outside the closet
door to the very end of the act. During that time, from the first
moment to the fall of the curtain, we have not only heard a
glorious succession of ensembles; we have also witnessed, years
ahead of its time, the birth of music drama!

Wolfgang Amadeus Mozart had made the acquaintance of
his librettist, the Venetian adventurer-poet, Lorenzo da Ponte, in
Vienna at the house of Baron Wetzlar, a musical amateur. Composition of "The Marriage of Figaro" was begun in the autumn
of 1785 and, according to da Ponte, took only six weeks. The
composer himself chose the subject, a popular play by Pierre
Caron de Beaumarchais (1732-1799) which had its public
premiére in Paris, April 27, 1784, after various injunctions by the

official censors. The Austrian Emperor Joseph II, who, like Louis XVI of France, had forbidden the play's production, at length consented to have the opera given in the National Court Theater and even permitted the inclusion of a ballet, which was at first forbidden. Mozart finished the Overture two days before the world première of May 1, 1786.

Michael O'Kelly, the Irish tenor who sang the first Basilio and Curzio at the age of twenty-four, under the name of Ochelli, described the première in his memoirs forty years later. "Never was there anything more complete than the triumph of Mozart and his 'Marriage of Figaro,' " he wrote, making special mention of the animation of Francesco Benucci as Figaro. Apart from Anna Salina Storace, the twenty-year old Susanna whose mother was English, and Nannina Gottlieb, the Barbarina, the entire company was Italian. Stefano Mandini was the Count; his wife the Marcellina; Francesco Bussani, who was also described by da Ponte as inspector of properties and costumes, doubled as Bartolo and Antonio. His wife, Dorotea, was the Cherubino. Laschi sang the Countess, and the composer conducted in crimson pelisse and gold-laced cocked hat.

Legend exists that "Le Nozze di Figaro" reached America as early as 1799 under the title of "Follies of a Day." Rumors of performances in May, 1823, in an English version by Sir Henry Rowley Bishop cannot be substantiated. The best evidence indicates that the American première took place at the Park Theater in New York on May 10, 1824, in English, followed by a melodrama, "Teresa, or the Orphan of Geneva." The cast was headed by a Mrs. Holman, who later appeared as Mrs. Sanford, in the role of Susanna; Miss Johnson as the Countess; and Mrs. Banker, born Miss Jones, as Cherubino. Mr. Pearman sang Figaro, and Henry Placide, Antonio.

A stellar cast presented "Le Nozze di Figaro" for the first

time at the Metropolitan Opera House on January 31, 1894, under the baton of the Neapolitan conductor, Enrico Bevignani. On this occasion Emma Eames sang the first of her twenty Metropolitan performances as the Countess. Lillian Nordica's delineation of Susanna was deemed "intelligent" by William J. Henderson of the Times; Mario Ancona was criticized as "deficient in grace and lightness" as Figaro; Edouard de Reszke made a "splendid" Count Almaviva and Sigrid Arnoldson a "most dainty" Cherubino. Emily Lablache was the Marcellina; Antonio Carbone sang Bartolo; Antonio de Vaschetti, Antonio; while the Messrs. Rinaldini and Mastrobuono were Basilio and Curzio.

DIE MEISTERSINGER VON NÜRNBERG

DURING the closing ensemble of the first act of "Die Meistersinger," the masters pronounce judgment over Walter von Stolzing and his trial song. "Versungen und verthan,"—"outsung and rejected," they conclude. Walther's song does not satisfy the rules which, in their opinion, must govern a work of art.

Many times in his own stormy career Wagner himself was judged in a similar manner by critics and public. The composer had to spend the greater part of his days fighting those who accused him of writing incorrect, faulty music. "Versungen und verthan" was indeed a chorus that in real life rang many times in the composer's bewildered ears.

As a matter of fact, Wagner had a far better musical training and technique than his critics gave him credit for. It was the originality of his approach which stood in the way of his immediate popularity. As he himself said, the listeners of his day expected elements in opera which he was not willing to provide. He wanted to present the elements of a great dramatic situation, but the public of his day was not used to this idea of music drama. They wanted pretty little tunes, smooth singing of conventional arias and songs. Above all they wanted to relax and be amused and entertained.

Wagner's music sounded strange to many of them because they didn't know what he was driving at. To many people first hearing Wagner's music, he seemed like an insane person whose torrent of musical words simply did not make sense.

165

The plot of "Die Meistersinger" is to a large extent a reflection of Wagner's own experience, his own struggle as a creative artist. Perhaps it is actually because the opera so closely mirrors Wagner's own sufferings, disappointments, and hard-won victories, that it is such an exciting, deeply human experience.

An autobiographical opera is unusual in operatic literature, but Wagner's basic problem is one that confronts every young artist in every generation: the conflict between new artistic ideas and old ones. The artistic ideas of the past are represented in the opera by the mastersingers, the older generation of settled, well-established citizens who believe in the academic rules that have been set and insist on respect for the traditions and forms inherited from the past.

These artistic ideas are also represented by a music critic, in the person of Beckmesser. When Richard Wagner created the character of Beckmesser he had one particular model in mind, the Viennese music critic Edward Hanslick. On several occasions Hanslick had pronounced severe judgment on Wagner's work, and the composer intended to take revenge by actually naming the ridiculous "marker" of the opera Hans Lick. It was with some difficulty that his friends succeeded in persuading Wagner to abandon that idea. And if Wagner painted in Beckmesser the caricature of his critical opponent, he undoubtedly painted a slightly idealized picture of himself in Walther von Stolzing. Who else could have been the model for this figure of an impetuous youthful artist whose genius breaks the rules of the past and eventually wins out over the petty criticism of Beckmesser and the mastersingers?

By identifying Walther and his fight against outworn artistic rules with Richard Wagner, however, we have not discovered the entire hidden meaning in the opera. When Wagner wrote "Die Meistersinger" he was already well past the early storms of his youth. In 1867 Wagner was fifty-four, no longer the young hero of his "Tannhäuser," "Lohengrin," and "Flying Dutchman" days. Thus Wagner does not limit his identification to the young Walther von Stolzing; he is also Hans Sachs, a person of a more mature, more settled character. Here is the man who values the flaming, soaring imagination as well as the established rules and the service they have rendered to the continued progress of the arts.

These rules, despite their extreme rigidity, did not hamper a genius like Wagner. Stolzing might not see why it should be so important to press a song into two verses of equal length, parallel structure and similar melodic content, two *Stollen,* as they are called in the rule books of the mastersingers, and why the two verses have to be followed by an *Abgesang,* an after song or chorus, double in length and different in material. Hans Sachs, however, as a mature artist, knows that lawlessness and chaos cannot be tolerated. His is the mission of reconciling the wildness of Walther's imagination with the orderliness of the traditional form, which Wagner studied carefully in the sixteenth century rule books of the Nuremberg mastersingers. The form so vigorously enforced in the opera, two short verses of equal length and a chorus, twice as long, is one of the oldest forms of poetry. The ancient Greeks used it, as do the Americans of today. Many a Broadway hit song utilizes the same form, two short verses of sixteen measures and a chorus of thirty-two measures.

A German Wagner expert, Alfred Lorenz, advances the astonishing theory that not only is Walther's Prize Song built in accordance with this rule, but that the whole opera "Die Meistersinger" follows the same pattern. The first two acts of "Die Meistersinger," he claims, are of equal length. According to him, they are the two verses, and the last act, the *Abgesang* or chorus, is twice the length of the two preceding acts. When "Die Meis-

167

tersinger" is performed without cuts, the first act lasts about ten minutes longer than the second. In comparing the acts, however, it seems logical to deduct the Prelude which, after all, introduces the entire work and not just the first act. Omitting the Prelude, which lasts about nine minutes, the first and second acts are nearly equal in length. The third act, the *Abgesang,* also uncut, is twice the length of the preceding acts, just as the rule book prescribes.

If we accept the theory, the first two acts, like two verses, must also follow a similar pattern of construction. Mr. Lorenz maintains that the first two acts do indeed show a far-reaching similarity of construction and even of content. The first act opens with a solemn church chorus, welcoming the eve of St. John's Day. The second act opens with a gay chorus of apprentices, celebrating the same eve of St. John's Day. During the chorus of the first act, we also witness a little love scene between Eva and Walther. A counterpart in the second act can be found in the silly chatter between the two other lovers, the apprentice, David, and Eva's nurse, Magdalene.

As a matter of fact, Lorenz claims that situations presented seriously in one act are frequently treated humorously in the other. For instance, we have Walther and Eva seriously in love in Act I, as soon as the curtain rises on the opening Chorale. In Act II Wagner depicts the love of David and Magdalene on the lighter side as Magdalene playfully scolds her young friend. By the same token the slightly absurd lesson in poetry that David gives Walther von Stolzing takes about the same position in the first act that Hans Sachs' famous *Flieder* monologue on poetry takes in the second. In the first act we hear Walther trying to win Eva. His examination song is interrupted by the marker's strokes, and the whole episode leads into a quarrelsome ensemble. In the second act somebody is again trying to win

168

Eva, only this time it is Beckmesser, also by a song, his Serenade. Again there are interruptions, now Hans Sachs hammering on the shoes, and another time a quarrelsome ensemble, the street-fighting scene at the end of the episode. The closing scenes of both acts show further resemblance. After all the noise and commotion everybody leaves; only one person remains on the stage: Sachs in the first act, the nightwatchman in the second.

Whether Wagner planned all this intentionally and deliberately made this whole opera into one gigantic mastersong, complete with two *Stollen* and an *Abgesang*, will never be established. What *do* we know about the secret workings of a genius? Wagner may not have used the form intentionally, but perhaps he was so filled with the ideas which he put into the great work that mysteriously and without a conscious plan the opera took on the form prescribed in the old rule of the master-singers. Whatever the theory is, a discovery of a master plan or an interpretation applied by posterity, it helps to clarify the structure of this tremendous work. "Die Meistersinger" is so great an achievement that we cannot ignore any ideas that might help us to penetrate its vastness. There are always new discoveries, new joys, new revelations in this immense opera from whose pages Wagner, the greatest mastersinger of them all, speaks to us not only with the flaming genius of Walther von Stolzing but also with the mature wisdom of Hans Sachs.

Richard Wagner, composer of both words and music, in 1835 visited Nuremberg, where he became involved in a tipsy riot which soon melted away, leaving Wagner and his brother-in-law, Heinrich Wolfram, to stroll peacefully through the moonlit streets. Ten years later, taking a cure at Marienbad with his wife, Minna, he recalled the Nuremberg street brawl and, with Gervinus' "History of German Literature" fresh in his mind, feverishly sketched the scenario of "Die Meistersinger." Two other prose sketches remain, both written in 1861 and both depicting Sachs as a mellow philosopher rather than the cynic of the first scenario. One of them also contains several pages of notes on the rules of the mastersingers which Wagner had culled from Wagenseil's "Nuremberg Chronicle."

The poem was written in thirty days during January, 1862, a bright period in Wagner's desperate existence in Paris, since he was able to share his enthusiasm with the Countess de Pourtalès, to whom he read the verses.

The music was begun in Biebrich, the Overture completed by April, 1862, before he had begun a note of the text. Working in appalling heat for eight hours a day, the composer was forced by financial difficulties to turn aside from composition and resume his concerts. Thus, he did not complete the score of "Meistersinger" until October 24, 1866, in his house Triebschen on Lake Lucerne. A piano arrangement was published the following year and the full score in 1868.

Hans Sachs, a leading character in the comic opera, was an historical figure, born November 5, 1494. He died January 19, 1576. He was married twice, first to Kunegunde Kreutzer (1519), then to Barbara Haescherin Endres (September 2, 1561). The action of the opera falls on June 24, 1561, during the cobbler poet's brief widowerhood.

After inspiring the orchestra and cast with a brief speech at the final rehearsal of "Die Meistersinger," Wagner attended the première at the Royal Court Theater on June 21, 1868, acknowledging the enthusiastic applause of the public from a box at the request of the King of Bavaria, who was present. He recognized Franz Betz as predestined for the role of Hans Sachs; Franz Nachbauer pleased him more each day in rehearsals for the part of Walther. Mathilde Mallinger he felt to be a charming Eva, while nothing, he believed, could be found to equal in originality the Beckmesser of Gustav Hölzel. Kasper Bausewein was the first Pogner; Karl Fischer, Kothner; Karl Schlosser, David; Sophie Dietz, Magdalene and Ferdinand Lang, the Nightwatchman. The other mastersingers were Karl Heinrich (Vogelgesang), Eduard Sigl (Nachtigall), Eduard Hoppe (Eisslinger) and the Messrs. Pöppl (Moser), Thoms (Ortel), Grasser (Schwartz), Weixlstorfer (Zorn), and Hayn (Foltz).

"Die Meistersinger" reached the Metropolitan on January 4, 1886, when Anton Seidl conducted, firing the entire cast with his zeal. Emil Fischer dominated the stage with his "picturesquely burgherish" Hans Sachs. The conductor's wife, Auguste Seidl-Kraus, made a plump but attractive Eva. Albert Stritt sang Walther; Marianne Brandt was Magdalene; August Kramer, David; Carl Kaufmann, the Night Watchman; Otto Kemlitz, Beckmesser; Josef Staudigl, Pogner. Other mastersingers were Emil Sänger (Nachtigal); Hermann Weber (Schwartz), and the Messrs. Dworsky (Vogelgesang), Lehmler (Kothner), Hoppe (Zorn), Klaus (Eisslinger), Langer (Moser), Doerfler (Ortel), and Anlauf (Foltz). Members of several German singing societies volunteered their services to augment the male chorus.

OTELLO

THE development of a leading character throughout the course of an opera or play is frequently the most absorbing aspect of the entire drama. We find ourselves less concerned with the actual incidents of the plot than with the effects of these happenings upon the hero or the heroine.

In "Otello," for example, the struggle which we follow takes place within the soul of a human being. In the first act the hero appears as a noble character, strong and gentle. The next two acts trace his gradual decay into the tortured madman he ultimately becomes. This is character development, or rather character degeneration on a colossal scale, and the demands of the title role on the singing actor who must portray this breakdown are overwhelming.

Unlike Shakespeare's play, in which the slow deterioration is reflected through a multitude of scenes, Boïto's libretto depicts three main stages in the process. In the first act Otello is still a noble hero; in the second, he begins to give way, and, in the third he has become a raging maniac!

With his accustomed skill, Verdi was able to compensate for this lack of opportunity to indicate the gradual break-up of his hero. In the introduction to the third act, for instance, he relies only on the orchestra to apprize the audience of what is taking place.

Every Shakespeare lover realizes that it is the poison of

172

jealousy, cunningly and subtly administered by Iago, which is responsible for the spectacular change in Otello. This change is clearly indicated both by music and text in the second act of the opera. But to show how this poison of jealous suspicion continues to work on Otello's mind during the interval between the second and third acts, Verdi employs an unusual and effective device. The slithering and winding theme which we hear near the beginning of the second act, is the very tonal costume of the green-eyed monster.

Having once established this symbol, Verdi proceeds to make further use of it. The introduction to the third act repeats and develops this pattern:

We see (or, rather, we hear) how green-eyed jealousy, having attached itself to Otello's mind, now takes possession of his emotions and ultimately drives him insane. In other words, Verdi both advances the action and portrays development of character while the curtain is down!

Another musical device employed by Verdi to illustrate a bit of characterization is introduced in the last act, when the composer assigns to the double basses a passage in which they play the lowest tone of which the instrument is capable. This effective orchestration symbolizes the fact that Otello has sunk to the lowest depths a man can reach!

174

For all his prodigal display of ingenuity, Verdi never squandered his resources and usually managed to keep some unexpended effect in reserve for use on a special occasion. In the introduction to the last act of "Otello," for instance, the sound of the English horn comes as a most delightful surprise, simply because the peculiar tone color of the instrument has not been heard previously in the opera.

In "Tristan and Isolde," Wagner summoned this same instrument for the well-known solo passage near the beginning of the last act. But the composer did not withhold the instrument until this moment. As extravagant as Verdi was frugal, Wagner used the English horn throughout the opera.

Perhaps the best example of Verdi's genius for squeezing the utmost out of available resources is his treatment of the so-called kiss motive, which is first heard in the love duet as Otello leads Desdemona into the castle, near the conclusion of the first act. At the composer's disposal are exactly three syllables, the word *un bacio*, a kiss—hardly enough, one would think, to hit the listener with its full import. Yet Verdi wants us to remember it and to identify it with Otello's love for Desdemona. So he contrives a unique welding of the orchestra and the voice. First the orchestra initiates the theme and only at its climax does the voice enter to complete it.

175

This theme of the kiss has been carefully planted in the first act and associated in our minds with an ecstatic moment. When we finally hear it again, at the moment of greatest tragedy, just before Desdemona's death, it echoes through our minds with immeasurably greater emotional force. Otello himself is moved to tears, as this theme recreates for him the joyous promise of the first act, and he laments the more bitterly the ironic and tragic outcome of his love.

In contrast to this climactic moment is the adroit means chosen by both Verdi and his librettist to indicate the drunkenness of Cassio in the first act. To convey the fogged state of Cassio's mind, the ingenious Boïto has him attempt without success to recall the tune of Iago's song, making him grope clumsily for the familiar air and flounder among Verdi's weary musical intervals.

Nothing could show the disorganizing effects of alcohol with more conviction.

Shakespeare himself is, of course, responsible for the chief contrast between the characters of Iago and Otello in the drama. Iago, in a sense, is the key to Otello's character, a static delineation of evil, a complex character, equally hypocritical and cynical at the beginning and at the end. Under his influence, monstrous things happen to Otello, and to understand these things one must understand Iago. Dramatically speaking, he is such a fascinating character that it is easy to realize why Verdi seriously considered calling his opera by the name of its villain.

"If I had to act the part of Iago," wrote Verdi to a friend, the painter Domenico Morelli, "I should make him long and lean with thin lips; small eyes—set, ape like, too close to his nose—and a head with a receding brow and large development at the back. His manner should be distracted, nonchalant, indifferent to everything, incredulous, smart in repartee, saying good and ill alike lightly with the air of thinking about something else. So, if somebody should reproach him for a monstrous suggestion, he might retort: 'Really?—I did not see it in that light—let us say no more of it.' A man like that might deceive everybody,

177

even up to a point his own wife. A small malignant fellow would put everyone on his guard and would take nobody in!"

Boïto for his part maintained that "the most vulgar error an artist can commit is to portray Iago as a demon, to give him a Mephistophelean mask or satanic eyes. Every word Iago speaks proves him a man—a villainous man but still a man. He should give the impression of a jovial and easy-going young man, young and handsome . . . Shakespeare says twenty-eight years old . . . One of Iago's cleverest tricks is the ability to modify his behavior according to the company in which he finds himself. He is hail-fellow-well-met with Cassio, ironic with Roderigo; with Otello he seems kind, obliging, devotedly humble; he is brutal and threatening with his wife, polite and obsequious with Desdemona and Lodovico."

This duplicity is perfectly mirrored in Verdi's music. While Iago speaks to Cassio, the orchestra is full of innocent-sounding flourishes:

Listening to this music we do not doubt that here is a pleasant and well-meaning fellow. But as soon as Cassio leaves the stage and Iago is left alone, these innocent flourishes are altered to reveal the basic wickedness of Iago's soul.

"Otello" remains as one of the most masterly examples of the function of music to underline the drama of human emotions and inform them with an intensity not present in the spoken word. This is indeed the essence of the art of opera.

A sketch for an opera libretto on Shakespeare's "Otello" was first brought to Giuseppe Verdi by Arrigo Boïto in the summer of 1879 through the agency of their friends Giulio Ricordi, the publisher, and Franco Faccio, first conductor of the opera who introduced the topic to the composer at the dinner table. "The chocolate venture," as the project was termed in the conspiratorial circle, developed slowly in the composer's mind, though by the following January he was writing to another friend, the painter Morelli, about the physical appearance of the characters. He had not set down a note by March, 1883, and was "in no hurry to finish it," he wrote to the baritone Victor Maurel, on December 30, 1885. By November 1, 1886, the music of "Otello" was completed, and the première was shortly announced for February 5, 1887, at La Scala in Milan. The occasion was an event of international interest. Maurel's Iago was thought superb by the critics of the London Times and Daily Telegraph; Francesco Tamagno's impersonation of the title role "almost as good" by the Times reviewer, but Romilda Pantaleone, who had been chosen by the composer for Desdemona, was felt less satisfactory in her role. Giovanni Paroli was the Cassio; Vincenzo Fornari the Roderigo; Francesco Navarrini the Lodovico; Napoleone Limonta the Montano; Angelo Logomarsini the Herald, and Ginevra Petrovich, the Emilia.

"Otello" was introduced in the United States at a performance in the New York Academy of Music on April 16, 1888. Cleofonte Campanini conducted, and his wife, Eva Tetrazzini, sister of the famous Luisa, sang Desdemona. The Roman tenor Francesco Marconi was the Otello; Antonio Galassi the Iago, and

179

other members of the cast included di Comis (Cassio), Jovine (Roderigo), Bologna (Lodovico), Maina (Montano), and Morelli (Herald). Sofia Scalchi, who had left the Metropolitan in 1884, sang Emilia.

On the evening of March 24, 1890, "Otello" was first presented at the Metropolitan Opera House in a special season organized by Henry Abbey to feature Adelina Patti. Mr. Abbey's first attraction, the "Vulcan-voiced tenor" Tamagno, who repeated his La Scala success as the Moor of Venice, was judged by the Times critic to be "an actor of uncommon power . . . one of the most manlike men that ever trod the stage."

Emma Albani, the great Canadian soprano who had married the impresario Ernest Gye, was hailed for the charm and exquisite vocalism of her Desdemona, while Giuseppe Del Puente, the Valentin of the opening night "Faust" sang Iago; Synnerberg was the Emilia. Armando Castelmary, who died tragically upon the stage a year later, sang Lodovico. Messrs. Perugini, Bieletto, and De Vaschetti were responsible respectively for the roles of Cassio, Roderigo, and Montano. Luigi Arditi, composer of the popular waltz "Il Bacio," was on the podium.

PAGLIACCI

MANY years ago there occured, in the Calabrian village of Montalto, in southern Italy, an incident to send tongues wagging in horror and amazement: an actor, crazed with jealousy, had murdered his wife after a performance. Such a crime of passion has always held a morbid fascination for the public at large, but what distinguished this case from many another seven-day sensation is the fact that the presiding judge at the trial was a gentleman by the name of Leoncavallo, whose son, Ruggiero, was destined to achieve fame as the author and composer of "Pagliacci."

The criminal case occurred during the composer's boyhood, but made such a profound impression on him that years later, when seeking material for a libretto, he recalled the incident and made it the basis for his popular opera. Leoncavallo's memory served him in good stead, for later the French playwright, Catulle Mendès, accused the composer of stealing the story from him and even went so far as to secure a legal injunction to stop a performance. When the facts of the Montalto case, which was a matter of public record, were laid before Mendès, he dropped the suit.

It was natural for the story to appeal to Leoncavallo. Realism was invading the opera house as well as the theater in the late 19th century. There was a growing passion for life in the raw, and this new, young, vigorous style of theater and music acted like a tonic on a musical world that was becoming a bit stale

181

with conventional romantic emotion. Here, for a change, were real people, earthy, passionate, and full of life.

The gist of the "Pagliacci" story can be recounted in a few words: a group of comedians every night enacts the age-old farce of the deceived husband who allows himself to be bamboozled by his wife and her lover. Confronted with a similar situation in their own real life, they stop acting like comedians, and speedily turn the familiar plot into bloody tragedy.

The composer makes his intention known from the beginning. In the prologue, Tonio tell us: "This is not just a play, this is as real as life itself. Under their poor flimsy garb, these actors are people of flesh and blood. We are to see not sham and make-believe but a portrayal of life itself."

It is this constant juxtaposition of theatrical pretense and real feelings, of artificiality and sincerity, which is the real subject matter of the opera. Musically, the distinction between the play and reality is brilliantly realised by contrasting the old-fashioned dance tunes of the play-within-the-play with the otherwise modern Italian style of music which represents reality.

This alternation of styles is apparent from the first moment Canio sets foot on the stage. He is in his clown costume, and, like a barker advertising his wares, he urges the crowd to attend the performance that evening. But the clown quickly becomes serious when the villagers jokingly warn him to watch out that in his absence Tonio, the other clown, doesn't make love to Nedda. "Believe me," Canio warns, "it would be much wiser not to play such a joke." He points to the theater and says: "Up there on the stage when the clown catches his wife with a lover, he delivers a funny sermon or even lets himself get beaten up, but if Nedda were really to deceive me, the story would end very differently." And here, the composer, by contrasting the old-fashioned dance tune with the real emotional feeling of the man, immediately points out to us the real substance of the work. A deceived husband on the stage is one thing:

But in real life things are different; here is Canio without his mask: the man, not the clown:

This contrasting of the music of make-believe with the music of reality is also found in Nedda's duet with Tonio. The deformed clown pours out his heart to Nedda, but she laughs and says: "If you want to make love to me, do it by playing the fool on the stage, tonight. But now, please spare yourself the trouble." And we find Tonio's pleas to be those of a man who is experiencing genuine suffering, not the assumed sorrows of an actor.

183

Nedda's cruel rebuff, on the other hand, is set to the music of the play which we hear during the comedy of the second act.

The composer then introduces an excellent bit of dramatic counterpoint by simultaneously combining Tonio's lovesick pleading and Nedda's stinging rejection.

184

Having thus prepared the audience by gradually introducing the basic theme of contrast, the composer is all set for the main event, so to speak. In the second part of the opera, as the villagers watch the harmless little comedy which is being enacted on the stage, we hear first a minuet:

Then a charming gavotte:

Thus, when Canio bursts out with his true feelings, his voice crashes through the quaint elegance of that music with the shattering force of a stone thrown through a window.

"No, I'm not a clown," he sings in anguish, "I'm a man, a foolish man who loved his wife to the point of madness but who will now take his revenge for this betrayal!" The music is miles away from the charming dance tunes of Harlequin and Columbine:

Nedda, becoming really frightened, tries to calm Canio and
resume the play. "I never knew you were such a fearful man,"
she sings, as the music attempts to get back into the world of
make believe:

Canio is not to be put off. And, just as his realistic passion
takes control of the stage picture, so Leoncavallo's own contemporary idiom seizes orchestra and players alike. Dance tunes are
forgotten, and life is reflected as it exists in our violent world.

As the Prologue promised, we have seen not an old-fashioned
comedy but true emotions of real human beings: love, anger,
hatred, jealousy, and their bitter consequences. The violence of
these emotions has been translated throughout into music that
is literally spine-tingling. In fact, it is this unbridled extravagance
and realism of emotion which is the generating force behind
"Pagliacci" and which has kept it, after more than fifty years,
still at the boiling point. If the day should come when human

187

beings are no longer subject to these basic emotions, then perhaps this music will cease to have meaning. But, short of that unlikely millennium, it looks as though it were here to stay!

****

Ruggiero Leoncavallo (1858-1919) was earning a miserable living by teaching and playing the piano in cafés when he was inspired by the success of "Cavalleria Rusticana" to take his two-act opera "Pagliacci," which had been ineligible for Sonzogno's one-act competition, to the same publishers that had assisted his colleague. The composer, who had failed to win public favor with the first section of an operatic trilogy on the Medici family, found himself famous overnight, but he never succeeded in duplicating the effectiveness of "Pagliacci," for which he wrote both words and music.

The première took place at the Teatro dal Verme in Milan on May 21, 1892, given special éclat by the interpreter of the role of Tonio, Victor Maurel, who had been instrumental in getting the work on the stage. The composer also assigned him the Prologue in front of the curtain, although it was originally intended for a tenor. The first Canio was Giraud; the first Nedda, Adelina Stehle; Mario Ancona sang the part of Silvio and Francesco Daddi was the Beppe. Some of the original success of the work must also be credited to the twenty-five-year old conductor, Arturo Toscanini.

Gustav Hinrichs presented the American première of "Pagliacci," conducting the work at the Grand Opera House in New York on June 15, 1893. The Polish soprano Selma Kört-Kronold, who had sung for him the first American Santuzza two years before, was the Nedda; Giuseppe Campanari the Tonio, and Montegriffo the Canio. Perry Averill sang Silvio, and Di Pasquali was the Beppe.

The following season "Pagliacci" was introduced to the Metropolitan public with Luigi Mancinelli on the podium on December 11, 1893. Nellie Melba was well received as Nedda; Fernando de Lucia sang Canio; Mario Ancona was promoted from his initial role of Silvio at the world première to the part of Tonio, while Victor Gromzeski sang Silvio, and Pedro Guetary, Beppe.

PARSIFAL

IF the world had obeyed Richard Wagner's intentions, "Parsifal" would never be heard at the Metropolitan Opera House in New York—or for that matter at any other theater than Wagner's own festival shrine. So solemn is the story of "Parsifal," so devotional much of its music, that Richard Wagner during his lifetime did not permit any performances of the work outside of the auditorium he had built for the exclusive presentation of his works in the little Bavarian town of Bayreuth. The composer permitted all his other works to be performed all over the world. But "Parsifal" he felt required a special atmosphere, an attitude of concentration and reverence on the part of the audience that could not be achieved in the hustle and bustle of everyday life. According to Wagner, only the special setting of Bayreuth would meet these needs. In a letter to his protector, King Ludwig of Bavaria, Wagner wrote " 'Parsifal' should never be produced merely for the entertainment of an audience."

Literally speaking, the world has not obeyed the wish of Richard Wagner. "Parsifal" is being performed all over the world. But, in a broader sense, his intentions are still being fulfilled. Wherever it is performed, be it in the quiet surroundings of Bayreuth or in busy New York, it is always presented and received fittingly, as the composer suggested in his subtitle, "A Stage Consecrational Festival Play."

What is it that makes "Parsifal" a unique experience? What gives it this special quality that has made its presentation traditional during Christianity's most sacred week? To be sure, there

190

is a close connection between Christian symbols and many elements of the story and music of "Parsifal." Near the end of the first act we hear the solemn music that accompanies the unveiling of the Grail, the cup from which Jesus supposedly drank at the Last Supper, into which Joseph of Arimathea received the blood of the Savior upon the cross. The theme of the Grail contains a direct quotation from the celebrated piece of liturgical music, the Dresden Amen:

During the last scene of the first act we also witness the ceremony of the supper in the temple of the Knights of the Grail, presided over by the unfortunate Amfortas. Disfigured in his body by a never-healing wound and in his soul by remorse that makes him unfit to fulfill the exalted obligations of his office, he cannot unveil the Grail and saturate the spirits and bodies of the knights with its powerful radiation. The ceremony of the supper contains many elements of the communion service, the Eucharist.

The transformation of the bread and the wine is accompanied by one of the basic musical themes of the work known as the Eucharist.

191

We also hear the theme that symbolizes faith throughout the work.

Another relic kept by the Knights of the Grail is the Holy Spear which once wounded Christ on the Cross. It is presented musically by this unforgettable theme:

The loss of the Holy Spear by Amfortas, the king and spiritual leader of the Knights, and its recovery by Parsifal is the very core of the story of this work.

These are some, but not all, of the roots which hold the story of "Parsifal" firmly in Christian soil. However, the work contains additional ideas which are akin to Christian thinking but not directly derived from it.

Wagner has also incorporated some of the great ethical concepts which were developed early in the nineteenth century

192

by the German philosopher Arthur Schopenhauer, whose writings made a deep and lasting impression on him. Schopenhauer's most important ethical principle is the idea of compassion as the basic element of human morals. The German word for compassion used by Schopenhauer, *Mitleid* (*mit*—with, *Leid*—suffering), means co-suffering, suffering with another being. According to Schopenhauer, this feeling of *Mitleid*, of compassion, the sharing of pain with others and the determination to alleviate such suffering, is responsible for every truly ethical, unselfish deed.

This principle of compassion as the source of all ethical behavior is contrasted by Schopenhauer with malice, an evil state of mind which finds satisfaction in the suffering of others. In "Parsifal" Wagner applied Schopenhauer's philosophical theories to the practical life of the stage. He created characters which clearly represent the opposing ethical principles of Schopenhauer: compassion and malice. The principle of malice is represented by Klingsor. Klingsor once tried to qualify as a Knight of the Holy Grail, but because his heart was not pure he was refused admittance. Ever since, he has been filled with rage and bent on vengeance. He has obtained the power of magic, has created a luscious garden in the wilderness and filled it with beautiful women who lure the knights from virtue.

As the opposite pole to the evil Klingsor, Richard Wagner has created the pure figure of young Parsifal. Listen to the rugged music that portrays the dangerous power of Klingsor.

What a contrast to the exuberant, noble music that represents Parsifal!

Parsifal is the ideal fulfillment of Schopenhauer's conception of a being guided by *Mitleid*, by compassion. It is not only that Parsifal wishes to alleviate the anguish of others. As the play progresses, he actually reaches a point where he suffers the pain of his fellow men in a mystic process of complete identification. Such a person must be pure in heart, he must feel the full impact of compassion, compassion with every fellow-being, and feel it by instinct, not through a process of reasoning or intellectual discovery. Before he even enters the stage, Parsifal is described as such a person. Gurnemanz speaks of the one that will come to heal Amfortas' wound and will restore the waning powers of the Grail. Help will come only from him who is, in Wagner's words, *ein reiner Tor*, a stainless fool. The German word *Tor*, however, does not mean a foolish person. It means rather a simple person, someone who is unspoiled. Parsifal's first act in the play is the senseless killing of a swan. As Gurnemanz reproaches him, Parsifal, in the words of the score, listens with growing emotion. As the old man asks him whether he does not realize the magnitude of his sin, Parsifal answers, "I did not know it was wrong." He did not know; he is, indeed, guileless. But comparison already has begun to make him aware. As Gurnemanz describes the suffering of the guileless animal, we hear the compassion theme:

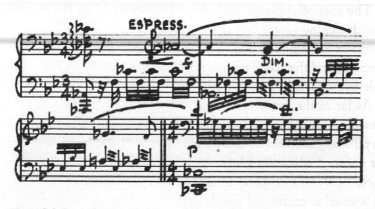

Parsifal breaks his bow and hurls his arrows to the ground. This is his first act of compassion. He will never kill wantonly again.

This new feeling of compassion takes rapid possession of the pure heart of Parsifal. It reaches a much fuller expression in the temple scene of the first act. Here Parsifal witnesses the bodily pain and mental anguish of Amfortas. As he hears the tormented man's cry of agony, he suddenly clutches his heart and, in accordance with Wagner's stage directions, remains in a petrified, motionless position as if he too would feel the pain of the wound. A more advanced state of compassion has now been reached: the process of identification with the suffering of another person.

Even this is not enough to give Parsifal the knowledge he needs to give him the powers that a complete realization of compassion will bestow on him. His purity, his ethical determination, have to be put to the test, as we see in the second scene of the second act of the opera.

When Parsifal enters Klingsor's magic garden he follows in the steps of Amfortas, who once came here to battle Klingsor only to be lured into the embrace of Kundry and to be defeated in his holy mission. Again it is Kundry whom Klingsor summons to conquer Parsifal.

Kundry is a strange figure, a creature torn between two worlds —the evil world of Klingsor and the pure world of the Grail. She is a woman who once laughed at Christ on the Cross and has been doomed ever since to wander until once more she finds a savior. She is temptress and comforter, demon and saint. Half-good, half-evil, she is devoted to the service of the Grail yet at the same time subjected to Klingsor's hypnotic powers, an unwilling yet ready tool of evil.

It is Kundry who is called upon by Klingsor when Parsifal approaches. The youth is now in exactly the same situation which once was fateful to Amfortas. While Amfortas was clutched in the embrace of Kundry, the Holy Spear was snatched from his hand by Klingsor. And, at that very moment when Kundry's lips touched his, Amfortas suffered the never-healing wound. This time it is Parsifal who sinks down in Kundry's embrace. Her arms around him, she is ready to touch his lips

196

with the kiss that will make him unworthy of his exalted mission. But at this moment Parsifal starts up suddenly with a gesture of intense terror. His looks alter fearfully, and he presses his hand tightly against his heart as if to repress an agonizing pain, exactly as he pressed his hand against his heart when he heard Amfortas' cry out of agony in the first act. Parsifal cries out, "Amfortas—the wound, the wound!"

This is a complete identification with another's pain. It is true *Mitleid*, co-suffering. Compassion has proved stronger than lustful desires. It is from this very act of compassion that Parsifal now derives his power. In resisting the lures of Kundry, in setting the image of the suffering Amfortas between himself and temptation, Parsifal has won the strength to vanquish the evil might of Klingsor.

Later in the third act, Parsifal returns on Good Friday to Montsalvat. Through compassion he has become worthy of assuming the highest office, the leadership of the knights. The exuberant and innocent young Parsifal is no more.

He has mellowed into a more serious, more mature, more knowing person.

197

He has returned with the Holy Spear. Thus, in the Grail scene of the third act, he restores the power of the Grail by healing Amfortas. But it is not the spear alone through which the miracle of the healing is accomplished. The power bestowed through compassion on the pure and simple soul has not only conquered evil but has washed away the wounds that evil has inflicted.

When Parsifal begins to take over his duties as spiritual leader of the knights, he once more reiterates the sources of his strength. And here again the music of the prophecy is heard.

Suffering and the full measure of compassion are the sources of goodness; not knowledge, wisdom, strength, or any qualities of the mind. Here the philosophy of Schopenhauer as projected by Richard Wagner is close to the basic teachings of many of the religious leaders of mankind.

In its last analysis, the whole story of "Parsifal" is already contained in a few simple words that were once spoken almost 2,000 years ago on a mountainside near the Lake of Tiberias: Blessed are the pure in spirit, for theirs is the Kingdom of Heaven.

198

As early as 1858 Richard Wagner confessed to the overwhelming emotion aroused by the fresh spring sunlight of a Good Friday morning, as he stood by a window at the Asyl, the guest house near their home outside Zurich offered to him and his wife Minna by the Wesendoncks. In 1865, settled comfortably in Munich in the house he had been given on the Briennerstrasse, Wagner had his studio upholstered in yellow satin, and pink and white satin draperies, with white tulle valances, and started to sketch the libretto to his last music drama. The plan was sent to his patron, King Ludwig, by the end of the summer, and a performance considered for 1872, but Wagner did not actually start the text based on the fifth and sixth books of Wolfram von Eschenbach's thirteenth-century poem, "Parsifal," until January 25, 1877, in Bayreuth. It was finished on April 19 of the same year and the music begun four months later.

The composition occupied Wagner until April 26, 1879. The orchestral score was begun on August 23, 1879 and completed on January 13, 1882, although the composer anticipated the conclusion by dating the final page December 25, 1881, as a gift to his second wife, Cosima. All the previous summer the initial cast was being assembled and the stage setting planned at Bayreuth, but it was at the Porazzi villa in Palermo, Sicily, where Wagner had gone to recover from a nervous disorder, that the "Parsifal" score was finished.

Back in Bayreuth on May 1, 1882, the composer busied himself with preparations for the première, which occurred on July 26, 1882, after three weeks of rehearsals. Hermann Levi, at first offended by Wagner's anti-Semitism, consented to conduct.

Hermann Winkelmann came from Vienna to sing the title role. Amalia Materna, who had created the "Siegfried" and "Götterdämmerung" Brünnhildes in Bayreuth, returned for Kundry. Theodore Reichmann was the first Amfortas and August Kindermann the first Titurel, neither artist being replaced in subsequent performances. Karl Hill was "a born Klingsor" according to Ernest Newman, and Emil Scaria's perfect enunciation as Gurnemanz pleased the local critic. The Flower Maidens, carefully trained by Lilli Lehmann and praised by the composer for their "faultless intonation," included Johanna Andre, Luise Belce, Carrie Pringle, and the Mmes. Galfy, Hors, and Meta. The four Esquires were Mmes. Galfy and Keil and Messrs. von Hubbenet and Mikorey. Anton Fuchs and Mr. Stumpf impersonated the Knights, and Mme. Dompierre sang the Voice.

"Parsifal" was first presented in the United States in a concert version conducted by twenty-four-year-old Walter Damrosch at the Metropolitan Opera House on March 4, 1886. It did not appear on the stage, however, until December 24, 1903, when General Manager Heinrich Conried flouted the objections of Wagner's widow, who wished to reserve the festival work for Bayreuth, and even defied a civil suit, as well as the outspoken prejudices of the clergy.

Although the conducting of Alfred Hertz did not suit all the critics, Mr. Krehbiel reported that Milka Ternina, the Kundry, "bewitched her audience with limpid song"; Alois Burgstaller proved "an admirable Parsifal"; Amfortas was "impressively sung and acted" by Anton von Rooy; and Robert Blass made "a creditable Gurnemanz." Otto Goritz made his debut on this occasion as Klingsor; Marcel Journet sang Titurel, and Louise Homer was heard as the Voice. The Flower Maidens included Isabelle Bouton, Marcia van Dresser, Florence Mulford, Elsa Harris, Katharine Moran, Lillian Heidelbach, and the Mmes. Braendle, Del Sarta, and Förnsen. The Knights were Julius Bayer and Adolf Mühlmann; the Esquires, Albert Reiss, Willy Harden, and the Mmes. Moran and Braendle.

PETER GRIMES

IN "Peter Grimes," with what at first glance seems to be an unpromising locale and a stark and somber subject matter, Benjamin Britten has succeeded in creating a masterpiece. The opera plays in a small fishing town on the east coast of England, in about the year 1830. It deals with two fundamental human problems: the conflict between an unusual man and the community, and the conflict between man and nature.

The grandiose way in which the sea dominates the atmosphere of the play is probably the most striking characteristic of the score. It is the spirit of the sea that is the real protagonist of the opera. A gigantic struggle takes place between the sea and this weird, austere, and visionary fisherman, Peter Grimes. One feels that although the ocean could destroy Grimes at any time it chooses to win him in its own way.

All Grimes' misfortunes are directly traceable to the power of the sea. The death of his first apprentice, which takes place sometime before the opera opens, is a direct act of malevolence on the part of the sea. We are told that Grimes was lured by the huge catch of fish, and no sooner did he sail the boat around the coast with the intention of putting into London than the wind turned against him and blew him off his course. For three days the sea kept him until the drinking water was all gone and the apprentice died.

The storm which starts at the end of the first scene and continues through the second causes a landslide and creates the precipice which is responsible for the death of Grimes' second

202

apprentice. Thus, the sea gradually drives Grimes insane until he finally commits suicide by sinking his boat in calm weather.

It is the music of the sea, now tranquil and cajoling, now threatening and terrible, that is the main glory of this opera. One might have thought it foolhardy to try and portray the sea in music after this subject was seemingly exhaustively treated by so many great composers of the past. Was there anything new that could be said after the sea storms of Mozart's "Idomeneo" or Verdi's "Otello"? Does the sea hold any musical secrets after Mendelssohn's "Fingal's Cave" or Debussy's "La Mer"? And yet such is the insight of the creative artist that Benjamin Britten's sea is completely unlike those of his predecessors and yet fully as beautiful as any of them.

In the first scene of Act I, on the borough beach, the sea is quiet. Gently and with monotonous regularity the surf beats against the shore, while the long notes in the violins and flutes sound for all the world like sea gulls. The sound of the C natural in the violins and flutes against the C sharp of the majestic A-major brass chord gives the peculiar effect of inhuman desolation and shows us again how a composer of exceptional musical sensitivity achieves extraordinary moods by using the simplest means.

There is no end to Britten's love and knowledge of the sea. The whistling of the wind, the gay whitecaps riding the waves,

203

the glitter of sunlight; all is there; nothing escapes Britten's eye and ear.

The other problem, the conflict between an unusual man and a community, is handled in no less masterful fashion. Grimes himself is a complex character: cruel yet poetic, an excitable visionary, a fighter and a dreamer. No wonder that the ordinary people of the borough have an instinctive suspicion and aversion where Grimes is concerned. Listen to his extraordinary soliloquy in Act I, Scene 2:

"Now the Great Bear and Pleiades, where earth moves, are drawing up the clouds of human grief, breathing solemnity in the deep night. Who can decipher in storm or starlight the written character of a friendly fate, as the sky turns the world for us to change? But if the horoscope's bewildering like a flashing turmoil of a shoal of herring, who can turn skies back and begin again?"

Grimes is answered by a chorus of: "He's mad or drunk!" The exceptional man is always thus greeted by his fellowmen. The anger of the borough against Grimes rises constantly throughout the opera and finds expression in the great ensemble of Act II.

205

In Act III the bitterness and hatred of his neighbors achieves an intensity of expression that is literally hair-raising:

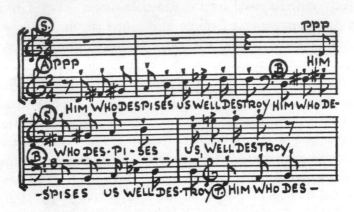

Those who have an opportunity to hear "Peter Grimes" can look forward to an unusual story told in a new and compelling musical language. Benjamin Britten accomplished in this work the fundamental aim of great art: to teach us something new about the human heart and express it through new and significant musical beauty.

Benjamin Britten re-read George Crabbe's poem, "The Borough" (1810), while working in California and experienced such nostalgia for his native Suffolk that he was soon fired with the thought of an operatic work based on the sea-coast tale.

The scenario was sketched by Britten with the help of the tenor Peter Pears. The novelist Montagu Slater wrote the libretto at a windmill at Snape which the composer had bought in 1938. Here the music was written, between concert engagements, from January, 1944, to February, 1945, three months after Britten's 31st birthday.

Although composed for the American stage, "Peter Grimes" was first presented at Sadler's Wells in London, on June 7, 1945. Peter Pears sang the title role and Joan Cross that of Ellen Orford, joining forces a year later with Messrs. Britten, Crozier, and Piper to form the English Opera Group which has been largely occupied with Britten's works. Reginald Goodall conducted a cast that included Frank Vaughan (Hobson), Owen Brannigan (Swallow), Valetta Jacobi (Mrs. Sedley), Edith Coates of Covent Garden (Auntie), Morgan Jones (Boles), Roderick Jones (Balstrode), Tom Culbert (Rev. Adams), Blanche Turner and Minnia Bower (the Nieces), Edmund Donlevy (Ned Keene), Sasa Machov (Dr. Thorp), and Leonard Thompson (Apprentice).

The American première took place August 6, 1946, at the Berkshire Music Center, Massachusetts, under the aegis of Serge Koussevitzky, who had originally commissioned the work. Leonard Bernstein conducted. The cast comprised William Horne as Peter, Florence Manning as Ellen, and James Pease as Balstrode. Leonard Treash was Swallow; Frances Lehnerts, Mrs. Sedley; Ellen Carleen, Auntie; Paul Franke, Boles; Paul Knowles, Rev. Adams; Mildred Mueller (latter Miller) and Phyllis Smith, the Nieces; Robert Gay, Keene; Byron Kelley, Dr. Thorp; and Frederic Zighera, the Apprentice.

The Metropolitan première took place on February 12, 1948, under the baton of Emil Cooper, evoking from the press such contradictory reactions as "the work has tremendous power . . . plenty of originality" (Miles Kastendieck, Journal-American), and "It adds nothing to the history of the stage or the history of music" (Virgil Thomson, Herald-Tribune).

"Frederick Jagel was excellent in the title role and Regina

Resnik was fine as . . . Ellen," wrote Douglas Watt in the Daily News. Philip Kinsman sang Hobson; Jerome Hines, Swallow; Martha Lipton, Mrs. Sedley; Claramae Turner, Auntie; Thomas Hayward, Boles; Lawrence Davidson, a Fisherman; John Brownlee, Balstrode; Thelma Altman, a Fisherwoman; the ill-fated John Garris, Rev. Adams; Paula Lenchner and Maxine Stellman, the Nieces; Hugh Thompson, Keene; Orrin Hill, Dr. Thorp; P. J. Smithers, the Apprentice and Lodovico Oliviero, the Lawyer.

THE RAKE'S PROGRESS

"THE RAKE'S PROGRESS," Stravinsky's latest stage work, is also his first full-length opera. The announcement that one of the foremost composers of our century was planning a major work for the lyric stage was greeted with joy, and the opera itself was awaited with impatience and understandable excitement. Nor was there any cause to feel disappointed. This is Stravinsky at his best, with all of his essential characteristics, even though they are presented in a somewhat simplified pattern and in a totally unexpected formal arrangement. Stravinsky discards in this opera all the trappings of the romantic and post-romantic era. Gone is the continuous music drama and the orchestra of symphonic proportions; gone are the leading motives and the everyday language of *verismo*. Like the bearded lady of the opera, they have been stifled by the white wig of rococo formalities. This is an unusual stylistic *tour de force*— modern content clothed in archaic forms, new wine in old bottles.

Just looking at the score, one feels Stravinsky's loving devotion to this 18th century milieu. On virtually every page, one encounters such Mozartian terms as aria, arioso, duettino, quartet, cabaletta, and stretto-finale. Nor is the composer merely parading old-fashioned titles. This is a real "number opera" with complete, individual pieces separated by recitatives, with "farewell" ensembles, prayers, and lullabies. The arias are constructed according to the time-honored principle of recitative, slow, fast. The voices regain their lost prerogative to indulge in flights of flexible fancies and some vocal cadenzas look almost as if they were lifted bodily from "Così fan tutte":

The gay epilogue of the opera, following the death of Tom Rakewell, is another typical 18th century feature. The moral, as a matter of fact, is the same as in the epilogue to Mozart's "Don Giovanni"—the classical warning of the dangers of sin. The choice of instrumental forces is an example of Stravinsky's well-known dedication to limited means and rigid self-discipline. This is an opera orchestra in the classical tradition, such as Mozart used in the "Marriage of Figaro": strings and harpsichord plus twelve wind players and timpani. Stravinsky even denies himself the use of trombones which Mozart added in "Don Giovanni." Occasionally, the flute and oboe are required to double on the piccolo and English horn, but then Mozart also permitted the piccolo to play a short passage in the second-act storm scene of his "Idomeneo." More 18th-century flavor is added by the use of the so-called *secco* recitatives, where the voices are accompanied only by the harpsichord. In the first scene of the second act, Nick Shadow, the evil one, describes Baba the Turk to Tom Rakewell and suggests that he marry her. Except for a few harmonic alterations, this could have come right out of a classical opera:

Stravinsky likes to mix orchestrally accompanied and *secco* recitatives, a special procedure which Mozart used, as far as I know, only in "Idomeneo." In the aforementioned conversation between Tom and Nick Shadow, Tom's lines are supported by the orchestra while Nick is accompanied by the harpsichord.

Here and there, Stravinsky takes advantage of the technical excellence of today's performers, in good twentieth-century fashion. Entrusting an entire introduction to a solo string quartet, as in the graveyard scene, or requiring the harpsichordist to play fairly complicated passages would have been considered too risky in the 18th century.

This is all very well, the reader will say, but the opera does not *sound* like an 18th century composition; it sounds much harsher, more nervous and complicated. No question about it. The contents are pure Stravinsky, and harshness, nervousness, and complication are characteristic earmarks of Stravinsky's style. The astonishing thing is that his very personal musical language adjusted itself so well to the conventions of a past century. As a matter of fact, in this atmosphere of refined simplicities, the individual features of the composer's style are, if anything, easier to perceive.

Distilled through the familiar conventional forms, the essential qualities of Stravinsky's vocabulary emerge with unusual clarity. The harshness which we mentioned is not the result of atonal or polytonal treatment, but comes from the simultaneous use of divergent harmonies within the same tonality. It is as if the accompanying chords were shifted around so that they appeared earlier or later than we would normally expect them. In the fast section of Ann Trulove's aria, for instance, we hear such a typical superimposition of tonic, dominant, and subdominant:

In its simplest and clearest way, this effect can be observed at that climactic moment in the graveyard scene, where Tom hears Ann's voice from backstage and realizes that love alone can save him from the clutches of the evil one:

The interesting feature of this Stravinskian dissonance is that, after a while, the ear becomes adjusted to it and reacts to this harshness with pleasurable recognition of the harmonic structure. We begin to unravel the telescoping harmonies, and in a strange sort of way learn to hear the same chords both simultaneously and in sequence.

What was at first merely strange and almost ugly begins to acquire beauty and meaning. The same process applies to that peculiar nervousness which has always been one of Stravinsky's most individual traits. The off-beat exclamatory chord is a typical mannerism of Stravinsky, and can be observed on numerous occasions in "The Rake's Progress." It is preceded often by what could be termed an "explosive silence" on the beat, somewhat similar to a sharp intake of breath:

The correct execution of these off-beat moments presupposes a great precision of muscular and rhythmical coordination, not unlike the "on toe" feeling of the classical ballet dancer. This alertness of body and mind is a prerequisite of Stravinsky's style and affects the listener as much as the performer. No wonder one does not relax while listening to this music. Even gently moving melodies, like the opening sentence of the quartet of the first act, acquire an iron-like quality through this off-beat device:

The setting of the English words in "The Rake's Progress" has given rise to some puzzlement. Reading through the score, one finds numerous places where the word-accent seems misplaced. It is true that the printed score shows a few oversights in regard to prosody which have since been corrected by the composer. But the general impression is based on a misunderstanding of Stravinsky's important technique of what we might call cross-meters. He often gives the vocal line a metric division which does not coincide with that allotted to the orchestra. In other words, the vocal accents do not always fall on the beat. When Ann sings the word "caress" in her aria at the end of the first act, the accent is not meant to fall on the first syllable of the word, even though the orchestral downbeat does come at that point. We simply are confronted with two lines of accents: one for the singer and one for the instruments. Far from being a

215

mistake, this is a fascinating and charming complication, a part of this new language of Stravinsky's which opera lovers will find more and more rewarding the more often they have an occasion to listen to it.

♪♪♪♪♪♪♪♪♪♪♪♪♪♪♪♪♪♪♪

Igor Stravinsky (1882-) states that for many years he harbored the idea of writing an opera originating in English prosody. In 1947, attending an exhibition of English paintings in Chicago, he was struck by the various series of William Hogarth (1697-1764) and later discussed problems of an opera in the English language with his friend and Hollywood neighbor, Aldous Huxley.

In September, 1947, Stravinsky informed his publisher, Ralph Hawkes, of his intention to write a full-length opera. Mr. Hawkes commissioned the English-born poet, Wysten H. Auden (1907-), who had been suggested to the composer by Huxley, to write the libretto. Two months later Auden joined Stravinsky in Hollywood and agreed with him on a three-act moral fable, based on "The Rake's Progress," drawing up a synopsis of plot, action, scenes, and characters. In New York Auden enlisted Chester Kallman (1921-) as his co-librettist and the text was completed by March, 1948. The composition occupied Stravinsky for three years.

The première of "The Rake's Progress" took place at the Fenice Theater in Venice on September 11, 1951, a highlight of the annual Venice Festival. Lord Harewood, editor of "Opera," referred to Elisabeth Schwarzkopf's characterization of the role of Ann Trulove as "beautiful" and noted her "complete musical command and accuracy." The Rake, Robert Rounseville, proved "a sad disappointment" to the same reviewer, while Jennie Tourel, "a delicate miniature," seemed to him miscast as Baba. Nell Tangeman was "a rather strident Mother Goose" but Otokar Kraus as Shadow "added another success to his gallery of portraits from Hell." Hugues Cuenod was praised for his brilliant singing as Sellem, the Auctioneer. Rafael Arie was "a competent Father Trulove" but the composer's conducting "had little to recommend it."

Criticism on the work itself was varied. The Venice Gazzettino spoke of "the rare balance and delicious clarity of the orchestral commentary." The Milan Corriere noted that "the confusion is general" but decided the evening was "a fiery success." Representatives from Liverpool and London called it "a disappointment" on the one hand and a "masterpiece" on the other. The Paris Figaro compared it to "Contes d'Hoffmann" and the Daily Mail to the work of Britten and Menotti.

Reactions at the American première, which took place at the Metropolitan Opera House on February 14, 1953, under Fritz Reiner, were equally varied. Virgil Thomson in the Herald-Tribune found the music "enchanting" and announced that the cast, headed by Hilde Gueden as Ann Trulove, Eugene Conley as Rakewell, and Mack Harrell as Nick Shadow, sang "impeccably." Olin Downes, commending Miss Gueden's "range and brilliancy" in the Times, still felt that "the opera remains a study in still-life," and compared it to a house of cards which could fall apart at a touch. Other members of the cast were Blanche Thebom, who was warmly applauded as Baba; Martha Lipton, an effective Mother Goose; Norman Scott as Trulove; Paul Franke as Sellem, and Lawrence Davidson as a Keeper.

217

RIGOLETTO

THERE is nothing in the history of art more fascinating to study than those periods in which men of genius rebelled against formulas accepted without question by their fathers and grandfathers, and created for themselves a new, fresh, and exciting world of beauty. From this point of view nineteenth-century opera can well be called a triumph of the romantic spirit.

The great opera composers of a hundred years ago were merely using the human voice, just as Keats, Shelley, Byron, Victor Hugo, and Pushkin used the pen. They were all excitedly engaged in kicking over the traces of formalism, in rediscovering the individual character in all its waywardness and contradictoriness.

In "Rigoletto" we see one great romantic teaming up with another, for the text of "Rigoletto" was derived from a play by the reigning king of the new literary romantics, Victor Hugo.

It is not hard to see how the story of "Rigoletto" fascinated the romantic temperament. It is full of bold, even garish contrasts of character. Rigoletto himself is a romanticist's dream hero. He is complicated, he is twisted both inside and outside, he drips with picturesque misery. He is good and he is bad. Rigoletto is a genuine, simon-pure, 99.44% product of the romantic creative mind. The more unusual and even pathological the character, the better Hugo and Verdi like it. Here we have a man who is physically monstrous, the romantics had a weakness for monsters; he is capable of infinite cruelty and callousness, yet he is also capable of the purest and most tender devotion.

218

This very complexity of character is in his favor from the composer's viewpoint, because a many-sided personality lends itself to many and varied musical facets.

Our first view of Rigoletto shows him taking a sadistic pleasure in rubbing salt in the wounds of Count Ceprano. Knowing the torments the Count is suffering because of the Duke's attentions to his wife, Rigoletto goes out of his way to demand with an elaborate air of innocence, "What is it disturbs our good lord of Ceprano?" He finds the Count's helpless but frantic concern a highly amusing spectacle.

Rigoletto's treatment of Monterone, the father of another of the Duke's young victims, is incredibly wicked and cruel. Taking advantage of a jester's privilege, he sneers at this unhappy father, and derides his concern for the virtue of his daughter.

Having in the first scene shown us Rigoletto the monster, the author now introduces us in the second act to Rigoletto the man. We are made to feel the utter misery of his life as a wretched misshapen jester, forced to be the laughing stock of the courtiers he despises. "I've been doomed to a life of evil," he says. He also makes us feel the tragedy of having had taken from him one of the two redeeming factors of his wretched life—his wife, the angel whose love was akin to pity. Now his only consolation is his daughter, on whom he lavishes all his affection and for whom he is ever fearful.

The crux of the whole story lies in the dramatic irony involved in the fact that Rigoletto's callousness toward another man's love for *his* daughter should apparently be the very instrument that eventually brings Rigoletto's own daughter to a tragic end.

The father's curse which Monterone calls down upon Rigoletto's head is, indeed, of such dramatic importance that Verdi originally intended to call the opera "La Maledizione," the curse. Actually the very first notes of the orchestral prelude to the opera sound forth the same impressive phrase that is so often sung by Rigoletto when he recollects Monterone's malediction.

Of the four times that the curtain falls, it does so three times to the accompaniment of a musical figure which depicts the working of the curse; a descending chromatic scale first at the end of the first act, when the curse has just been pronounced; again at the end of the second act, when Rigoletto discovers that he has assisted in the abduction of his own daughter; and, of course, at the very end of the opera when the curse is fulfilled.

The broad irony continues. Rigoletto, who had never permitted himself to be swayed by the sufferings of others, must himself appeal for compassion, and to the very men he had so cheerfully wronged.

Nineteenth-century romanticists got their effects by overstatement and violent contrasts. And yet, despite the poetic justice involved in Rigoletto's tragedy, we feel deeply for this character, particularly in the third act, when he comes to the palace frantically searching for his daughter, Gilda.

Although he is in an agony of apprehension, he must play the clown as usual and feign indifference as the gentlemen of the court mock at him. When he realizes beyond a doubt that his daughter is in the palace, only the intervention of the courtiers can keep him from breaking in on the duke. "Give me my daughter," is his agonized cry. "You have had your triumph. Let me see her. Stand back, I say!"

Rigoletto, as the central character, naturally shows the many-sided temperament so dear to the heart of the romantics. But even such a relatively minor character as Sparafucile, the professional assassin, is not painted entirely black. He has pride in his profession. He offers a neat workmanlike job, satisfaction guaranteed, for only fifty per-cent down. And, once he has undertaken a job, he aims to see it through. When his sister pleads that the Duke's life be spared, he is highly indignant. He has already accepted Rigoletto's down payment on the job of despatching the Duke. How can he go back on his promise? What does she think he is, a *crook?* The man is quite aghast at his sister's suggestion that he murder Rigoletto instead. "Have you lost your senses?" he demands. "Have I ever double-crossed a client?"

And yet Sparafucile also has a sentimental streak in him. Like many a tough hombre he becomes weak-kneed and soft at the sight of a woman's tears, and it doesn't take the sobbing Maddalena long to persuade him to kill a substitute, should one appear before midnight.

Our young heroine, Gilda, can similarly boast of many contrasting elements in her character. She may be impersonated all too often as a typical antiseptic operatic blond, but she is no hapless, namby-pamby heroine. Having given her heart, she gladly sacrifices her life for a man who is quite unworthy of such devotion.

We meet her first as she greets her father with the simple joy of a young girl, but already in the "Caro Nome," that touching oath of eternal constancy, we admire her determination to be true to her love until her last breath. This is no superficial crush of a moonstruck adolescent. In the last act she proves the sincerity of her pledge, when she offers herself as a victim to the assassin's dagger. When it comes to the final test, Gilda shows cool courage and resolution. She dies willingly, asking her father's forgiveness for what she has done, asking also forgiveness for her betrayer.

At times we may be tempted to smile a little at the violence of the emotions so typical of this romantic period; but it is easy to make fun of these stories only as long as we read them in the sober words of a storyteller. The moment the magic chemistry of great music touches these happenings, everything is transformed, even our own realistic, critical sense. Verdi forces us to believe in the sincerity of the emotions portrayed and accept the joys and sorrows of his characters as our own.

First of the operas by Giuseppe Verdi to win a permanent place in the standard repertory, "Rigoletto" was composed in forty days during the autumn of 1850. On March 9th of the same year Verdi had signed a contract with the Fenice Theater in Venice for a new opera. His choice of Victor Hugo's play, "Le Roi s'Amuse" (1832) as a subject was accepted with some misgiving by the theater, though the composer was assured by his librettist, Francesco Maria Piave, that there would be no objections from the censor. On December 1 the new opera, under the title of "La Maledizione," was prohibited altogether by the military government of Venice. Verdi at first refused any modifications but finally consented to change Francis I of France into an unnamed Duke of Mantua, to rechristen Triboulet as Rigoletto, and to remove the other characters from the realm of French history to that of sheer Italian fiction.

"Never was sound more eloquent," wrote the critic of the

Gazzetta di Venezia, commending "the novelty of phrase and cadence" and "the originality of their general contours." Meanwhile "La donna è mobile" became the tune of the town.

Tho firot "Rigoletto" performance, on March 11, 1051, was conducted by the composer. The part of the jester was taken by the baritone Felice Varesi, who had also served as Verdi's first Macbeth. The Duke was Raffaele Mirate, while Teresa Brambilla, who later married the composer Ponchielli, sang Gilda. The rest of the cast comprised Mmes. Casaloni, Saini, Morselli, and Modes Lovati as Maddalena, Giovanna, the Countess, and the Page, respectively, and the Messrs. Pons, Damini, Kunerth, Zuliani, and Bellini in the roles of Sparafucile, Monterone, Marullo, Borsa, and Ceprano.

Max Maretzek conducted the first American "Rigoletto" on February 19, 1855, at the Academy of Music, where his wife, Bertucca Maretzek, sang the role of Gilda. Amalia Patti-Strakosch, sister of the great Adelina, was the Maddalena, while Ettore Barili, her half-brother, sang the title role. The remainder of the cast comprised Biagio Bolcioni (Duke of Mantua), Luigi Rocco (Sparafucile), Colletti (Monterone), Muller (Marullo), Quinto (Borsa), Leonardi (Ceprano), Barattini (Countess), and Avogadro (Giovanna).

The first Metropolitan "Rigoletto" was offered under the baton of Auguste Vianesi on November 16, 1883, with Roberto Stagno, repeating his successes as Manrico and the "Puritani" Arturo, in the role of the Duke. Luigi Guadagnini sang Rigoletto, and Sofia Scalchi, Maddalena, while young Marcella Sembrich made her seventh appearance of the season as Gilda. Other members of the cast were Franco Novara (Sparafucile), Achille Augier (Monterone), Amadeo Grazzi (Borsa), Baldassare Corsini (Ceprano), and Mmes. Genelli, Forti, and Goldini as the Countess, Giovanna, and the Page.

THE RING OF THE NIBELUNG
DAS RHEINGOLD

I T IS difficult, if not impossible, to find in any realm of art a work even remotely comparable to this musical colossus, Wagner's Ring of the Nibelung. But sheer size, however breathtaking, cannot be its own justification; and as we examine Wagner's "Ring" we discover that his extravagance of means is born of the conviction that nothing less would do. The Wagnerian demands on the orchestra, on the singers, and on the producers are not the most severe he could think of, but rather the minimum that would do justice to his artistic conception.

Consider the orchestra; Wagner radically enlarged the number of instruments for the "Ring." The "Rheingold" orchestra includes sixty-four strings and thirty-six wind instruments. The most spectacular increase is in the brass section, which is practically doubled and also augmented by the then newly-invented tenor tubas. The purpose of all of this expansion, however, is not merely to secure a great volume of tone. Much more important is the matter of tone color. With a sufficient number of instruments of the same type available, Wagner can write in harmony for a group of similar instruments and thus achieve a *unified* tonal color otherwise impossible. In the old orchestra, the Valhalla motive, for example, would probably have been assigned to horns, trombones, and a bass tuba. Now, however, Wagner is able to obtain his desired sound by writing this music for tubas alone.

Wagner specifies no less than *six* harps in the orchestra pit, plus a seventh on the stage to accompany the Rhine maidens at the close of the opera. But here again is instrumental extravagance not for its own sake, but for a unique effect near the end of the opera. Wagner uses these six harps to describe the shimmer of the Rainbow Bridge leading to Valhalla. Notice to what lengths he goes to get the exact effect he is after; the six harps do not simply double each other by playing in unison; Wagner writes a separate and different musical line for each of them. To give you some idea of how little Wagner spared himself, let me point out that this involved writing out as many as 216 notes *per measure* for the harps alone!

But even the six harps do not provide the full measure of glistening irridescence Wagner wants, so he puts his enlarged choir of violins to work. Again he is not content to let the instruments merely double each other but divides his thirty-two violins into eight groups of four violins, and for each of these groups he writes distinct and separate parts, no two of which are alike. This means an additional 144 notes per measure, so that the total of harps plus violins brings us to the astounding figure of 360 notes per measure. And this, mind you, just for the *accompaniment*, the shimmer effect, while the motive proper of the Rainbow Bridge is played by other instruments.

Wagner's extravagant instrumental demands are not limited to the orchestra players in the pit! For the scene in the Nibelheim smithy, Wagner specifies that eighteen anvils be placed about the stage. These anvils are allotted *nine* different rhythmic patterns and require the services of eighteen extra musicians on stage to do the hammering correctly.

This colossal instrumental apparatus has certain dangers, of course, and Wagner was well aware of them. He was not only a great creative author and composer, but also a daring innovator in the fields of operatic production and stage direction. He considered the clarity of the sung word the most important single element in opera, and took special precautions lest the singers be drowned out by this gigantic orchestra. In designing his theater at Bayreuth, therefore, he arranged for the orchestra to sit in a sunken pit that actually extends under the stage, so that the sound of the more powerful instruments is kept subdued.

This pit is built in six levels, the top one being occupied by the conductor and part of the strings, while the remainder of the orchestra is distributed on the lower levels so that the loudest brass and percussion instruments sit well under the stage.

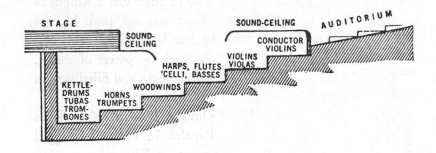

Cross section of Bayreuth Orchestra

It becomes, in effect, an invisible orchestra, for Wagner was concerned not only that the orchestra should not drown out the singers but also that the sight of this immense orchestral apparatus should not distract the attention of the audience from the stage picture!

Wagner was responsible for numerous other scenic innovations; he insisted that the auditorium be darkened during the performance and introduced the theater curtain which parts in the middle instead of being pulled up and down: the type that is now used in almost every opera house. All these means— the invisible orchestra, the auditorium in the form of an amphitheater without side boxes, the darkened house, the so-called Wagner curtain, contributed to the same goal: the presentation of opera as musical *drama*.

He demanded historical accuracy in the costumes and singers who knew how to act. Each of these was to be not just a vocal automaton but a characteristic individual. Wagner, furthermore, insisted on a high degree of realistic illusion in his fire, water, and cloud effects. To show the Valkyries riding through the sky he used a magic lantern—at a time when gas lighting was only beginning to be used in the theater!

In this day and age he would undoubtedly have employed moving pictures for this effect. In fact, his use of moving scenery in "Rheingold" and "Parsifal" anticipated the techniques of Hollywood.

All too often one hears it said that in Wagner it is only the orchestra that counts. Nothing could be further from the composer's own ideas and desires. It is the union, not the separation, of all its elements, auditory and visual, from which the music drama of Wagner derives its greatest vitality!

In developing his epic tetralogy, "The Ring of the Nibelung," Richard Wagner had recourse to two legendary sources which

227

he studied in the 1840's. These are the Norwegian "Volsunga Saga" of the 13th century and the Austrian "Nibelungenlied," which the composer knew in the editions of Lachmann, Grimm and Hagen. From this material he devised a detailed prose sketch of the entire drama, which was concluded on October 4, 1848, in Dresden, where he was serving as musical director of the Saxon Court.

On the basis of this sketch and the scenario which he completed on October 20th, Wagner first wrote the poem "Siegfried's Death," "a grand heroic opera in three acts" which we know today as "Götterdämmerung." Next came the extended prose sketch for "Rheingold," which he made between March 23 and 31, 1852, in Zurich, where he had fled because of his participation in the revolutionary activities of 1849. The "Rheingold" poem was completed in November, 1852, after that of "Die Walküre."

Unlike the poems, the music of "The Ring" was composed in the chronological order of the music dramas. Inspired by a creative revery he had experienced on a trip to Spezia, on August 4, Wagner began the music of "Das Rheingold" on November 1, 1853, completing it on January 14, 1854, and finishing the orchestration the following May 28. He was living in Zurich, composing only in the morning, and spending many of his evenings with his friends, Otto Wesendonck and his wife, at the Hotel Baur au Lac. It has been computed that he must have completed about five pages each day, using score paper for three or four staves, on which the vocal line was interwoven with the orchestral in pencil.

The première of "Das Rheingold" occurred on September 9, 1869, at the Royal Court Theater in Munich in the absence of the composer, whose growing romance with Cosima Liszt, the wife of Hans von Bülow, made him unwelcome at the Bavarian capital. Not only did von Bülow resign his post as Kapellmeister in June, 1869, but Wagner's disciple Hans Richter, von Bülow's successor, withdrew on August 28 rather than risk a performance of "Das Rheingold" without the composer's sanction.

King Ludwig II, bent on presenting the first "Rheingold," finally secured a capable chorus director, Franz Wüllner, known also as a composer and pianist, to conduct the première. The performance was first scheduled for August 25, but was postponed three times and finally took place on September 22, with two repetitions on the 24th and 26th. August Kindermann sang Wotan. Heinrich Vogl and his wife, Therese Thoma, impersonated Loge and Wellgunde. Anna Kaufmann sang Woglinde, and Fräulein Ritter, Flosshilde. Sophie Stehle, who was to sing the first Brünnhilde the following year, was Fricka; Karl Heinrich, Donner; Franz Nachbauer, Froh; Karl Schlosser, Mime; Kaspar Bausewein, Fafner; Karl Fischer, Alberich. The cast also comprised Mr. Petzer (Fasolt) and the Mmes. Seehofer (Erda), and Müller (Freia).

Anton Seidl, who had assisted Wagner with the score of the "Ring," was in charge of "Das Rheingold's" first presentation at the Metropolitan Opera House on January 14, 1889, when the work established the record of nine performances in a single season. Max Alvary, as Loge, reminded Henry Krehbiel unfavorably of Beckmesser on this occasion. Emil Fischer graduated from his original Alberich to Wotan. Twenty-two-year-old Sophie Traubmann sang Woglinde, sharing the Rhinemaiden functions with Felicia Kaschowska as Wellgunde and Hedwig Reil, who sang both Flosshilde and Erda. Ludwig Mödlinger and Eugen Weiss impersonated the giants Fasolt and Fafner. The rest of the cast comprised Alois Grienauer (Donner), Albert Mittelhauser (Froh), Joseph Beck (Alberich), Wilhelm Sedlmayer (Mime), Fanny Moran-Olden (Fricka), and Katti Bettaque (Freia).

229

DIE WALKÜRE

Whether we are at the opera or at a football game, one thing must be decided: whose side are we on? It is human nature to take sides, to identify ourselves with the characters in the drama—usually with the most important character, since our inner emotional reactions are not troubled by undue modesty! The audience's sympathy for the hero and the heroine is something on which the dramatist counts and capitalizes.

At a *Walküre* performance everyone in the audience is rooting, so to speak, for Siegmund and Sieglinde. And, lest there be any doubt about it all, Wagner promptly makes a musical bid for our sympathies in behalf of the young lovers; the hero is bold and handsome, the heroine is both beautiful and unhappy, their love is tender and passionate, and the husband is a black-hearted scoundrel.

The audience decides at once that the husband, Hunding, is a villainous wretch, and that the Goddess Fricka, who is on his side, is nothing but an old shrew, a tiresome, nagging kill-joy.

The facts, of course, would seem to indicate that Hunding is a respectable member of the community, a substantial citizen, and property-owner. He has been called on by his friends to help chase an outlaw. When he returns to his house, he finds a stranger who has walked in and made himself at home without so much as a by-your-leave, and is already making eyes at his wife. This stranger turns out to be the very outlaw the husband

and his posse have been pursuing. Even so, Hunding acts in an honorable manner: he tells the newcomer to defend himself in combat the next morning, and warns him to respect the sanctity of his home. The gentle heroine in the meantime manages to put a sleeping potion into her husband's nightcap, and when Hunding wakes up the next day he finds that the outlaw he treated so honorably has robbed his house of its most precious possession, his wife! How would you like it? Even the fact that the lovers are brother and sister doesn't seem to prejudice the audience against them. In real life, people undoubtedly would react quite differently, but from their seats in the opera house they are cheering the young couple on and not worrying very much about right and wrong.

It is, of course, only fair to mention that Sieglinde had some justification for her behavior: she was forced into marrying a man she has never loved. But what reason can Wotan offer in the second act for killing Hunding in cold blood? Is it not strange that the spectators in the auditorium seem to approve of this unprovoked and unnecessary murder?

Still, we mustn't be too harsh with the listeners. After all, they react the way it was intended that they should. Wagner, through his musical magic, makes Sieglinde and Siegmund appear to be in the right, while conventional virtue, in the person of Hunding, is not made very attractive by the composer.

Hunding is always given a raven black wig and a fierce-looking beard and make-up; his manner is gruff, and he stalks about making himself unpleasant. However physically attractive Fricka may be, and she *is* a regal figure on the stage in her flowing robes, she does not seem very pleasant either. Right is certainly on her side, but she is ill-tempered and petulant. Wotan, of course, is a tragic character, yet his best friend would have to admit that his marital transgressions have been considerable, and Fricka loses no opportunities to remind Wotan of what she has been through! She is not the type to suffer in silence!

Thus, Wagner stacks the cards outrageously in favor of the young lovers, and it is not surprising that the audience is all on their side, exactly as he intended. Their love scene in the first act belongs to the most glowingly rapturous musical utterances in the entire operatic literature!

In the second act, too, Wagner makes not only a sympathetic but a heroic figure of Siegmund when he defies Wotan's daughter, Brünnhilde. Learning that he is to die but that Sieglinde must be left behind, Siegmund calmly but resolutely refuses to follow Brünnhilde. "You are young and beautiful," he declares, "but you are heartless. My sorrow may not touch you, but do not try to lure me with the empty delights of Valhalla."

Thus Wagner plays amazing tricks with the audience of "Die Walküre." Somehow he sees to it that when we enter the opera house we leave the world of reality and enter an imaginary and overwhelming world of sound and feeling. The universe created by the power of music becomes momentarily more persuasive than the cold logic of our everyday conventions!

Richard Wagner outlined the prose sketches of "Die Walküre," "The Valkyrie," between the eleventh and twelfth of November, 1851, in Albisbrunn, a hill town southwest of Zurich, Switzerland, where he had gone for a water cure. In May, 1852, he and his wife Minna went halfway up the Zurich Berg for a new cure. Here, in spite of incessant rains, the composer-librettist finished the poem on July 1, 1852.

Composition of the music was begun on June 28, 1854, in Zurich, but Wagner was interrupted to conduct Beethoven's Seventh symphony at Sion, in Valais, in mid-July. After Sieglinde's exclamation: "Guest, who thou art I fain would learn," he scrawled in the score: "Answer when I get back from Sion."

The composer took up the threads again on August 3 and finished the first act September 1. Three days later he began the second act, which he completed November 18. The third act he began on November 20 and finished December 27.

In March, 1855, Wagner undertook an unfortunate trip to London, where he made little progress with the scoring of "Die Walküre," although his friend Karl Klindworth (whose adopted daughter, Winifred, married Richard's son Siegfried in 1915) enthusiastically began a piano score. The scoring of Act I was finished on April 3, 1855; Act II at the beginning of October in Zurich, and Act III on March 23, 1856, while the composer was suffering from painful chronic attacks of shingles.

Unlike the later "Ring dramas," "Die Walküre" was first performed at the Royal Court Theater in Munich, under the patronage of King Ludwig II and the baton of the Westphalian conductor, Franz Wüllner. In spite of the opposition of the composer, who wished to reserve the work for a future festival theater (Bayreuth), "Die Walküre" was presented, after twenty-five stage rehearsals, on June 26, 1870, in the presence of such celebrities as Joachim, Brahms, and Saint-Saëns. The King remained at his castle, Hohenschwangau. Wagner was living at his retreat, Triebschen, on Lake Lucerne.

The roles of Siegmund and Sieglinde were appropriately filled by the recently married couple, Heinrich Vogl and Therese Thoma. The tenor, a former elementary school teacher, was noted for his powerful voice but designated by Wagner as "thoroughly incompetent." Sophie Stehle, the "Rheingold"

233

Fricka, sang Brünnhilde. The Wotan was August Kindermann, who was to be a member of the first Wagnerian touring company twenty years later. Kaspar Bausewein was the Hunding and Anna Kaufmann the Fricka, and the Valkyries were the Mmes. Lenoff, Ritter, Deinet, Müller, Tyroler, Seehofer, Eichheim, and Hemauer. The work made a deep impression and was hailed by the local Neueste Nachrichten for its "gigantic talent."

Adolf Neuendorf, who had also introduced "Lohengrin" to New York, conducted the first American "Walküre" on April 2, 1877, at the Academy of Music. The Siegmund, Alexander Bischoff, was pronounced "unimaginative" by the Graphic. The Post reported that Alouin Blum "looked the part of Hunding to perfection." The Times maintained that Felix Preusser filled the role of Wotan "with appropriate dignity." The Herald criticized Mme. Listner for her "semi-inaudibility and stage awkwardness." Pauline Canissa, as Sieglinde, was described as "conscientious and forcible" by the Times, and the Post declared that Eugenie Pappenheim, the Brünnhilde, delivered her difficult part "with apparent ease and freedom." In spite of bad weather, the audience was both large and prompt.

Leopold Damrosch introduced "Die Walküre" to Metropolitan Opera House audiences on January 30, 1885, a fortnight before his untimely death. Amalia Materna, who had been chosen by Wagner for the first Brünnhilde in his festival theater at Bayreuth, repeated the role. Anton Schott was praised by William J. Henderson of the Times for his unexpected *cantabile* delivery of Siegmund's Love Song. Josef Koegel, a Bayreuth alumnus, proved capable as Hunding. Josef Staudigl was equal to the task of Wotan, in Mr. Henderson's opinion. Marianne Brandt, "self-sacrificing as usual" in the words of Krehbiel, doubled as Fricka

234

and Gerhilde. The other Valkyries were the Mmes. Kemlitz, Robinson, Stern, Brandl, Morse, Slach, and Gutjar. The production was thought by Mr. Krehbiel "the crowning achievement of Dr. Damrosch and his artists."

SIEGFRIED

IN creating the character of his hero, Siegfried, Wagner was under the sway of an ideal that was by no means new. In the preceding century, the French philosopher Jean-Jacques Rousseau had proclaimed the doctrine of the noble savage, the uninhibited natural man, unencumbered and uncorrupted by the trappings of civilization. This unsophisticated, natural nobility was supposed to furnish solutions to every conceivable human problem and to provide the foundations of a new social and moral order, a role which Wotan prescribed for his Wälsung offspring.

Siegfried displays a variety of characteristics, some admirable, some objectionable. His most obviously appealing attribute is his youthful vitality, his sheer love of life, as depicted in this rugged theme in the first act:

Another attractive trait is his eagerness for adventure. The whole wide world is waiting, and he exults in his sense of freedom.

Siegfried possesses not only physical strength, but a strength of purpose as well. When he is given the broken sword of his father, Siegmund, he does not try simply to weld the two pieces together, but grinds them down to powder and forges the sword

236

anew. He is capable of sustained effort to achieve his ends; he has vigor, resolution, and thoroughness.

Not only has Siegfried a good deal of natural wit and reasoning power; certainly his loneliness, his longing for a mother, are sympathetic facets of his character. Wagner makes this doubly true with a tender theme as Siegfried lies in the woods, daydreaming about his mother.

On the other hand, Siegfried shows a nasty, sadistic streak. He is not above abusing his strength for the fun of terrifying someone who is weaker. He finds it highly amusing to set a bear on his foster-father, Mime, and watch the little fellow shake with fear. It is true that Mime is a despicable character who has fostered Siegfried for the sole purpose of slaying the dragon, Fafner, and winning the ring and the gold for himself. Still, Siegfried's reasons for hating Mime seem singularly repugnant. He has learned that the clear stream acts as a mirror, because he has seen the images of the animals accurately reflected. He has seen his own appearance, illustrated by the Wälsung theme:

Compared to his own image, Mime is like a toad:

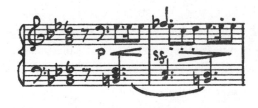

237

In other words, Siegfried hates Mime because he *looks different,* has different features from his own. Anything different is obviously inferior, according to the master-race philosophy.

In the beginning of the third act, when Siegfried meets his own grandfather, Wotan, we again find Siegfried in one of his less endearing moments. It is true that the young hero is not aware of the identity of the Wanderer, but even so his treatment of the stranger, to whose age at least he should show respect, is rude and brutal.

In the final scene at the Valkyrie rock, after Siegfried has broken through the flames, the youth once more proves himself highly sympathetic. Indeed that final scene of "Siegfried" shows a remarkable emotional development for both Siegfried and Brünnhilde. We last saw Brünnhilde at the close of "Die Walküre" when Wotan kissed her into a deep slumber. Up to that moment she was a proud Valkyrie warrior maiden, serving her father, Wotan. In "Siegfried" the goddess becomes a woman and the boy becomes a man. Siegfried has never known fear, but looking for the first time upon Brünnhilde, a woman, he at last meets a power stronger than himself. A new dimension is added to his personality.

Brünnhilde is also at the threshold of an overwhelming experience: life as a mortal being. She solemnly greets the light of day on her awakening, but she remains unaware of the implication of what lies ahead. Brünnhilde cannot at once surrender her ties to the past. While Siegfried gazes on her in feverish excitement, Brünnhilde sadly surveys the remainders of her lost godhood: her horse Grane, her shield, and her spear. She feels herself a helpless, defenseless woman, and she draws back in terror when Siegfried tries to embrace her. In Valhalla no god has dared to touch her. She buries her face in her hands with shame at her fallen estate, but here Siegfried shows a surprising tenderness. He draws her hands gently away and begs her to take courage from the smiling, sunlit day. When still she pleads with him to leave her, Siegfried continues his passionate pleas, urging her to awaken and be his. Brünnhilde recognizes that to yield to mortal love is to surrender her serenity and godlike wisdom forever. Still, she does so, wondering that Siegfried is not afraid of her own tempestuous feelings. Their closing duet reaches new heights of exaltation as the emotional turmoil each has felt gives way to sheer ecstasy.

An amazing transformation takes place in the course of one scene: Brünnhilde, the goddess, embraces life and is no longer aloof and superior to it, while Siegfried, in whom neither dragons nor fire could inspire fear, surrenders like any weaker mortal to the overmastering power of love.

This is Siegfried the hero at the apex of his humanity. If he has been harshly treated by the public, it is because of resentment that, with all his failings, he has been set up by Wagner as an ideal. Because he is human, he is destined to ultimate failure in the high mission of salvation for which he has been appointed. He comes closest to true nobility in the final, glowing moments on the Valkyrie rock. And if he achieves his finest hour because of a woman's love, that makes him no less a hero and perhaps even more a human being.

〰〰〰〰〰〰〰〰

The myth of Siegfried, which has nothing to do with the downfall of the gods in ancient mythology but was woven into the epic by Wagner himself, occupied the composer during the late spring of 1851. The twenty-seven-page prose sketch was made between May 24 and June 1 in Zurich. Two days later he started the poem, completing it by the 24th, but not finishing the necessary revisions until December, 1852. In his autobiography, Wagner tells of reading it to a small group of friends late in December at Mariafeld near Zurich, after breakfast, having finished the "Rheingold" and "Walküre" verses at midnight the preceding evening! Within a few weeks the dramas were printed in Zurich at Wagner's own expense and circulated to his friends.

It was not until September, 1856, that Wagner undertook the composition of "Siegfred," which occupied him at irregular intervals until June 14, 1869, the full score being completed on February 5, 1871. During this period Wagner took up residence with his wife, Minna, in the guest house of the Wesendoncks near Zurich. Here he laid aside "Siegfried" to write "Tristan" in 1857. In 1861 having broken with his wife, he travelled to Vienna to hear "Lohengrin" for the first time, visited Paris, and completed "Die Meistersinger." On August 25, 1870, he married Cosima von Bülow, shortly after completing the first-act sketch of "Götterdämmerung."

The première of "Siegfried" was postponed by Wagner's desire to create his own festival theater where his works could be performed under his personal supervision. He therefore refrained from sending the score of "Siegfried" to King Ludwig on its completion, as he had contracted to do in 1864, and withheld its publication although plans for a Munich première had been ordered by the monarch.

After innumerable delays, the first consecutive performances of "The Ring of the Nibelung" were held at the new Festival Theater in Bayreuth in August, 1876, with King Ludwig present at the final rehearsals from August 6-9. The première of "Siegfried" took place on August 16 lead by thirty-three-year old Hans Richter, who conducted three cycles. The title role was taken by George Unger, a gigantic tenor from Mannheim whom Wagner paid to study at Bayreuth for an entire year, the composer himself teaching him to act. The Wanderer was Franz Betz, "an admirable singer but a mediocre actor," said Saint-Saëns, while the role of Alberich was entrusted to the nervous Karl Hill, whom Wagner had to quiet with champagne. Lilli Lehmann had high praise for Karl Schlosser's "excellent" Mime, and Wagner himself applauded the inexhaustible vocal endurance of Amalia Materna as Brünnhilde. Franz von Reichenberg, from Stettin, was the Fafner, and Marie Haupt sang the Voice of the Forest Bird, although Lehmann had prepared for it. Luise Jaïde of Darmstadt, whom Cosima Wagner scolded for her table manners, was the Erda.

The first Metropolitan "Siegfried" was presented on November 9, 1887, independently of the other dramas of the cycle. Mr. Krehbiel hailed the "love, knowledge, devotion and enthusiasm" of Anton Seidl, who conducted, the "thrilling power" of Lilli Lehmann as Brünnhilde, the "splendid vigor and freedom of movement" of Max Alvary as Siegfried, and the "excellent impersonation" of Mr. Ferenczy as Mime. Emil Fischer's Wanderer was described as "splendidly musical and dignified," while Rudolf von Milde "did as much as possible" with the role of Alberich. Marianne Brandt was the Erda, and the Voice of the Forest Bird was sung by Auguste Seidl-Kraus, the wife of the conductor.

GÖTTERDÄMMERUNG

PERHAPS the most significant characteristic of Richard Wagner's music is the use of descriptive melodic phrases or themes called *Leitmotive*, a word which musical guidebooks usually translate as "leading motives." These motives are fairly simple, short, melodic phrases which are heard whenever certain ideas, characters, or objects are mentioned or seen. Sometimes these motives are vocal melodies and seem to derive from speech inflections, like the motive of the adoration of the Rhinegold, joyously sung by the Rhine maidens:

Most of the motives, however, are allotted to instruments rather than to voices. The sword motive, for example, is a typical trumpet figure.

Motives may have a rhythmic origin, like the motive of the anvils of the Nibelheim:

The shape of a melody may also have significance. Notice how the motive of the ring goes down, then up again to complete the circle, producing the rounded form of a ring:

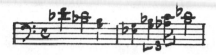

To be certain that we do not miss something of importance, Wagner often prepares us in advance by musical allusions to things to come. For example, in the first scene of "Rheingold," at the bottom of the Rhine, the initial appearance of the motive associated with the glint of the gold shining in the sun is sounded by the trumpet at the precise moment when the rays of the sun strike the gold with their full brilliance. But, in order that this musical moment may have its maximum effect, Wagner has familiarized us with the melody a few pages earlier in the score, when the light of the sun starts to penetrate the murky depths. It appears underneath the musical rippling of waters, and is sounded by one French horn:

Soon it is presented by two horns, and finally by three. We are thus prepared for the big moment:

When a firm relation between the motive and its meaning has been established in the listener's mind, he learns to recognize quickly and almost unconsciously what the composer is driving at. The power of association takes over, and Wagner uses it subtly and effectively to give the audience important

243

information which words and action alone couldn't possibly convey.

A striking example of this procedure occurs in the first act of "Tristan und Isolde," when Wagner through his orchestra clarifies the meaning of the words and makes his own comment on the proceedings directly to the audience. As the ship nears the shore, Isolde proposes that she and Tristan share a drink of atonement, to bury the past. The voices of the sailors cause Tristan to look about and ask, "Where are we?" Isolde answers: "Near the goal." Ostensibly she means the English coast, but the music that accompanies her words is the death motive:

This tells us unmistakably that the goal to which she is referring is something quite different, namely the death of both Tristan and herself!

The leading motives can also fulfill an important story-telling function when the character himself is *not* visible on the stage. In the second act of "Die Walküre," for example, we are informed by purely musical means that Hunding is in hot pursuit of the two fleeing lovers. We *hear* him in pursuit, long before we *see* him!

Actually, the use of this device did not by any means spring entirely from Wagner's brain. It was a creation of the German romantic era of Wagner's predecessors. Wagner, however, did bring the system to its fullest flower even if he didn't plant the seed. His intensive use of leading motives influenced at least two generations of composers in all fields of music, not in opera alone.

Later, there developed a considerable reaction against this method of composition. Debussy ridiculed Wagner's idea as being a kind of an audible visiting card, presented every few minutes by the guest, even after he has been introduced! There were complaints about the too obvious use of leading motives, particularly when they tell us nothing new. If Siegfried is brandishing a sword, those critics pointed out, we hardly need to hear the motive to know it is a sword! Others asked why the motives had to be repeated over and over again to the point of redundancy.

But one wonders whether the more subtle use of motives would be possible unless they were first established firmly in our consciousness and implanted there by obvious and continuous repetition. Apparently that was the composer's own experience with this technique. In "Tannhäuser," an early work, when he was feeling his way toward an effective system of leading motives, Wagner missed fire at one point simply because a motive had not been sufficiently established beforehand. In the prelude to Act II, the mood of festivity is supposed to be threatened by an ominous reference to Venus' curse.

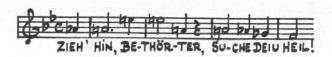

However, it fails to come off, because the music of the curse itself is only casually indicated in the first act, and we simply do not remember it as being Venus' curse.

If the Wagnerian method of motives has a disadvantage it is that of a certain ineffectiveness without a vast canvas and a great

245

deal of time not only to present the motives but also to fix them in the mind of the listener by constant repetition. It took a man of Wagner's magnificent courage and vision to conceive the truly colossal scheme of writing four music dramas dealing with the same story and based on related musical material. Here, for once, there was enough time to present all the necessary motives and to impart to the audience a complete vocabulary of musico-dramatic associations. In "Götterdämmerung" Wagner reaps the benefit of this vast indoctrination. By the fourth evening the listeners can follow a narrative told in purely musical terms without benefit of any visual or verbal clarification. The orchestra can at last take over large segments of the story, like a massive Greek chorus commenting on the action.

Wagner the dramatist and Wagner the musician rarely worked together with so much common purpose as in the purely instrumental sections of "Götterdämmerung." Think of the magnificent Rhine Journey, the prelude to the third act, or the stupendous Funeral March, not to mention the closing scene of the opera when, following Brünnhilde's singing of the Immolation, the orchestra depicts the final moments of the drama, the downfall of the gods. The Rhine Journey and the Funeral March sound well as concert pieces, but it is only in relation to the content of the entire tetralogy that their full emotional impact is revealed.

The great virtue of the motive scheme is that it works two ways. It not only foreshadows the future but, by evoking the past, gives the present an infinitely greater poignancy. There is no point at which the advantage of Wagner's system is so apparent as in Siegfried's Funeral March in the third act. The whole "Ring" cycle seems to pass in review while the vassals carry the dead hero back to the Hall of the Gibichungs.

We relive all the important moments of Siegfried's history.

246

It is as though Wagner were saying: "Remember the Wälsungs, the race of free men, free agents, who were to resolve the wretched dilemma of the cursed gold? Remember in "Walküre" the meeting of Sieglinde and Siegmund, their love, and its bitter pain?" By combining their love theme with the motive of woe, Wagner makes it clear to us that they were doomed from the start. "Remember the magic sword which Wotan had driven into the tree for Siegmund to claim? Remember how Siegmund and Sieglinde produced the hero, Siegfried, who grew to magnificent manhood and achieved his appointed meeting with Brünnhilde?" Over all the story broods the Curse of the Ring which means destruction for all who touch it.

Wagner felt all men to be creatures of destiny; even Siegfried, the free hero, could not escape his fate. But an even more basic thesis of Wagner's philosophy is that you cannot escape the theater. It has its own unwritten laws as meaningful as any written commandments. And making the audience participate through association of ideas is perhaps the most important of all theatrical laws!

The poem entitled "Siegfrieds Tod" (Siegfried's Death), which eventually became "Götterdämmerung" ("The Twilight of the Gods"), was begun by Richard Wagner in the autumn of 1848, as soon as he had concluded the sketch for the entire Nibelung drama. In deference to the criticism of his friend Eduard Devrient who felt the audience would not understand the plot, Wagner prefaced the Gibichung scene with the colloquy of the Norns and the scene between Siegfried and Brünnhilde. Early in 1849 he drastically revised the script but did not achieve its present form until December, 1852. A number of tentative musical fragments were drafted between 1848 and 1853.

The actual composition of "Götterdämmerung" occupied Wagner at intervals from October 2, 1869, until November 21, 1874 when the instrumentation was completed. During this period, he married Cosima von Bülow, began the publication of his collected writings, and moved to Bayreuth, where he built his home Wahnfried and started the Festival Theater. Ill health was also mentioned by Wagner to King Ludwig II of Bavaria as another excuse for delaying and a reason why the "Götterdämmerung" Prelude could not be sent him as a Christmas present in 1869, and he gave 1871 as a possible date for its conclusion. But, although Wagner was working on the score of "Götterdämmerung" at his home, Triebschen, on Lake Lucerne during the spring and summer of 1870, he was in no hurry to finish the work, wishing to reserve it for the opening of his festival theater and to safeguard it from a performance in Munich over which he could not have full control. Its completion was celebrated by a Christmas fete at Wahnfried for which he added the final bars of "Götterdämmerung," the Redemption by Love motive, to a children's piece he had written in praise of Cosima.

The première of "Götterdämmerung" concluded the first "Ring" cycle on August 17, 1876, at the Bayreuth Festival Theater. George Unger was less satisfactory as Siegfried than in the previous opera, but Wagner gave generous praise to Karl Hill as Alberich and Gustav Siehr, the Wiesbaden bass who had learned the role of Hagen in two weeks. As Gunther, Eugen Gura was "really magnificent," said Lilli Lehmann, who herself sang Woglinde, with her sister Marie as Wellgunde and Minna Lammert as Flosshilde. Mathilde Weckerlin, who had pleased

Wagner as Elsa in Hannover, was the Gutrune, while Luise Jaïde later replaced by Marianne Brandt, sang Waltraute. Amalia Materna continued her exposition of the three Brünnhildes in all three cycles. The three Norns were the composer's niece, Johanna Jachmann-Wagner, Josephine Schefsky, the gossipy protegée of King Ludwig, and Friederike Grün, whom the composer later engaged for his London concerts. Hans Richter conducted, driving Wagner into a state of nerves with his rigid tempi.

"Götterdämmerung" reached the Metropolitan some nine weeks after "Siegfried," again conducted by Anton Seidl, on January 25, 1888. The Norn and Waltraute scenes were omitted. Lilli Lehmann's "vocal gifts and capabilities seem as inexhaustible as her zeal," wrote Henry Krehbiel in the Tribune, praising "the strength and sensuous beauty of her voice" as Brünnhilde. "The warmth and vigor" of Albert Niemann's art were also noted. (The tenor was fifty-seven at the time.) Adolf Robinson was the Gunther, Emil Fischer the Hagen, and Rudolf von Milde sang Alberich. The conductor's wife, Auguste Seidl-Kraus, was the Gutrune and the Rhinemaidens were Sophie Traubmann (Woglinde), Marianne Brandt (Wellgunde), and Louise Meisslinger (Flosshilde).

DER ROSENKAVALIER

WHEN opera was born it was a deadly serious affair, with little if anything to provoke a smile. The earliest operas dealt only with the most tragic and pathetic situations, enacted by a solemn crew of heroes, kings, gods, and goddesses.

When comedy finally entered the opera house it made its way by the back door. In the first half of the eighteenth century, operatic composers decided to provide amusing trifles to be performed between the acts of serious operas. These were called *intermezzi*, or intermission works. The practice actually was borrowed from the spoken stage, where songs, dances, even juggling acts were introduced as *divertissements* between the acts of a drama.

Some of these operatic *intermezzi* became extremely popular for themselves, and one of the most famous, Pergolesi's "La Serva Padrona," can still be heard frequently today. The immediate success of these *intermezzi* soon led to their elaboration, and, before long, the full-length *opera-buffa* was born. In choosing the plots for the average *buffa*, the librettists leaned heavily on the typical half-improvised comedy of masks, the Italian *commedia del arte*. The traditional clowns, Arlecchino, Brighella, Colombina, and Pantalone were lifted bodily, humorous situations and all, and set to music. The jealous husband, the ridiculous old man in search of a young wife, the conniving servants, the ludicrous spinster, the comic policeman; all of these became the stock in trade of every librettist. For centuries people laughed at these personalities and continue to do so today.

Even so distinguished a poet as Hugo von Hofmannsthal, who

provided Richard Strauss with the text of "Der Rosenkavalier," did not consider it beneath his dignity to take a few stock characters from the pages of the old Italian comedy.

Baron Ochs is an example of the amorous old fool. In Annina and Valzacchi we see the clever and unscrupulous hirelings. The pompous policeman of the last act is dignified only by his title of Commissary. Faninal, the typical newly-rich snob, is the same familiar type which we know from Molière's "Bourgeois Gentilhomme."

The music of Richard Strauss contributes enormously to the characterization of these types. The Baron, for instance, is made impossibly gross and overbearing, a pompous old wind-bag.

The scheming intriguers are both light-footed and light-fingered.

251

The policeman has a highly inflated sense of his own importance:

The old joke of having a man masquerade as a woman is played to the hilt, not only in the action, but almost more so in the music. When young Octavian camouflages himself in the attire of a servant girl, his music also goes into disguise. The heroic theme of the romantic young lover is transformed into a delightfully feminine Viennese waltz.

This sure-fire effect is later combined with another situation that has been bringing the house down for centuries: the drunk scene. This happens in the last act, when Octavian, again disguised as the maid Mariandel, pretends to get tipsy, and Strauss embroiders this episode with some delightfully tipsy music. The Baron plies Octavian with wine to the accompaniment of a sentimental waltz:

When the Baron tries to kiss Mariandel, he is suddenly impressed with her resemblance to the troublesome youth, Octavian. And the music underlines the shock moment just as a punch line accents the modern gag.

253

Another comic device is the portrayal of two contrasting episodes taking place at the same time and gaining humor thereby. At the opening of the second act, Sophie's stupid old duenna, Marianne Leitmetzerin, falls all over herself with excitement at the prospect of Sophie's marriage to a real aristocrat. She is impressed by everything to the point of hysteria, and babbles on ridiculously. In contrast to this worldly old piece, we hear the music of the serious, high-minded little Sophie who can only pray for divine guidance on entering the holy estate of matrimony. An even more spectacular use of contrast occurs during the love scene, near the close of the first act, when the tenor's florid aria is interrupted by a squabble between Baron Ochs and the notary over the terms of the marriage contract. Ochs wishes an entire castle and country estate deeded to him. When the tenor resumes with his second verse, the Baron and the notary continue their conversation. The Baron's demands happen to involve a legal impossibility. Balked in his ambition, he loses his temper, bangs on the table, and . . . stops the singer!

It is natural for us to expect the music of the orchestra to be appropriate to what happens on the stage, but Strauss goes beyond that and injects touches of subtle humor by making the orchestra contradict the words of the characters on the stage. In the first act, the Marschallin apologizes to the Baron for having kept him waiting, and assures him that she was suffering from a headache; the orchestra, however, roundly contradicts the great lady, and reveals quite clearly that it was rather Octavian's lovemaking that caused the delay!

MARSCHALLIN

ICH HAT-TE DIE SEN MORGEN DIE MI — GRÄ -NE.

In the levee scene, later, the animal vendor proclaims that the little puppies he is selling are house-broken. Alas, the music informs us immediately that his little charges are calling him a liar!

HUNDERLN SO KLEIN,

STACC.

HUNDERLN SO KLEIN UND SCHON ZIMMERREIN.

In a sense, the entire comedy takes place in the orchestra pit just as fully and completely as it does on the stage. There is a

255

graphic precision in the tone-painting of Strauss that almost rivals the vividness of the visual picture. It is true that Richard Wagner brought about a closer connection between the instrumental sound and the happenings on the stage than had ever previously been achieved, but in Strauss this development seems to reach its final point of refinement to date.

After the success of "Elektra," Richard Strauss again put himself in touch with the librettist Hugo von Hofmannsthal, who drafted the scenerio of "Der Rosenkavalier" in February, 1909. Discussions proceeded until the autumn of 1910, but Strauss was so pleased with the project that he started work on the music of the first act on May 1, 1909 before the text of the other two was ready, and even wrote music, in his enthusiasm, for the words *"diskret vertraulich,"* which Hofmannsthal intended as a stage direction. The poet did not recognize the central significance of the Marschallin's character until June, 1910, and the opera was originally to have been called "Ochs."

Rehearsals for the Dresden première began in January, 1911, but further modifications were demanded by the Berlin Intendant, George Hülsen-Haeseler, to suit the squeamish tastes of the city.

The première at the Dresden Hofoper took place on January 26, 1911, after Max Reinhardt had been summoned to whip the performance in shape and Alfred Roller had come from Vienna to supervise the scenery. This prejudiced the Dresden critics who, like their colleagues in Berlin and Munich, gave grudging approval to the work. They disapproved of its length,

256

its lack of unity, and its patchwork style. The London reviewers, however, hailed "Rosenkavalier" as a successor to "Figaro."

The first Marschallin, Margarete Siems, appears to have dominated the performance, but the first Ochs, Karl Perron, was later compared unfavorably to the Viennese baritone, Richard Mayr. Eva van der Osten was the first Octavian and Karl Schiedemantel the first Faninal. Minnie Nast sang Sophie; Riza Eibenschütz, Marianne; Hans Rüdiger, Valzacchi. The two Major Domos were Anton Erl and Fritz Soot, the latter also singing the aria of the Tenor. The other roles were taken by Ludwig Ermold (Notary), Josef Pauli (Innkeeper and Animal Vendor), Elisa Stunzner (Milliner), Alexander Trobisch (Flautist), Theodor Heuser (Lackey), Jan Trojanowski (Hairdresser), Edward Schindler (Philosopher), Sidonie Korb (Noble Widow). The three Orphans were Marie Keldorfer, Gertrude Sachse and Paula Seiring. The conductor was Ernst von Schuch.

"Der Rosenkavalier" was introduced to America under the baton of Alfred Hertz at the Metropolitan Opera House on December 9, 1913. The "style and diction" of Frieda Hempel, who had sung the Marschallin at the Berlin première, were commended by William J. Henderson of the Times. Margarete Ober brought authority and warmth to the role of Octavian, and Otto Goritz proved a satisfactory Ochs. Anna Case was the Sophie; Hermann Weil, Faninal; Rita Fornia, Marianne; Albert Reiss, Valzacchi; Marie Mattfeld, Annina. The Major Domos were Pietro Audisio and Lambert Murphy; the Orphans: Rosina VanDyck, Louise Cox and Sophie Braslau. The rest of the cast comprised Carl Schlegel, (Commissary), Basil Ruysdael (Notary), Julius Bayer (Innkeeper), Carl Jorn (Singer), Jeanne Maubourg (Milliner), Ruth Weinstein (Negro Boy), and Ludwig Burgstaller, who mimed the role of Leopold, the lackey, without interruption for nearly forty years.

SALOME

WHAT a subject for an opera! An oriental ruler consumed with lust for his own step-daughter, who also happens to be his niece; the maiden, an innocent virgin of sixteen, developing a compulsive desire for the attentions of a religious ascetic and, when thwarted in her wishes, moving heaven and earth to have the man decapitated so that she can satisfy her longing by kissing the lips of his severed head!

No wonder that at its first appearance, Strauss' "Salome" was considered perverse, nerve-racking, even monstrous.

The music, far from softening this morbid subject, seemed to magnify and underscore every lurid detail, clothing its magnificent depravity with every shimmering hue available on the palette of the modern hundred-piece orchestra.

For sheer nervous tension, this work far surpasses anything previously created. The audience is led from horror to horror while the expectation of impending doom pervades the atmosphere from the moment the curtain opens. Strauss delights in jangling the nerves of the listeners with strident and terrifying dissonances. The next moment he lulls them into security with the most mellifluous harmonies, only to strike out again with new tonal clashes. This mixture of harmonic styles forms one of the most fascinating aspects of the score.

Strauss himself justified this unusual technique by the need for strong contrast between the characters of Herod and Jokanaan, but warned against its indiscriminate use.

In creating the morbidly neurotic mood of "Salome," Strauss is greatly helped by the imaginative text of Oscar Wilde. The symbolic references to such natural phenomena as the moon and the wind are used by the composer to full advantage. The moon, whose brightness illuminates the scene from the first, continuously mirrors the underlying tensions of the drama. The unconscious yearnings and neurotic fears of the characters are symbolically revealed by their attitude toward the moon. Only the prophet Jokanaan, whose spirit dwells in the contemplation of the sunshine of religious truth, is untouched by nocturnal light.

Almost as soon as the curtain rises, immediately following Narraboth's wonderful phrase, "how beautiful is Princess Salome, tonight," the Page remarks that the moon is "like a woman arising from a tomb." But the love-sick captain of the guard, Narraboth, disagrees. For him she is "a little princess whose feet are like white doves . . . one might imagine she was dancing . . . " To Salome, fleeing the covetous glances of her stepfather, the moon is "a silver flower, cool and chaste." The superstitious Herod finds that she is like a "drunken woman reeling through the clouds," while the imperturbable Herodias, steeped in vice and impervious to omens, remains unmoved: "No, the moon is like the moon, that is all." Near the end, as Salome is lost in the contemplation of Jokanaan's head, the moon disappears behind clouds. Herod is seized with terror— "Put out the torches . . . hide the moon, hide the stars," he commands the servants. And here, in the dimness of the night we half witness, half guess the revolting climax of the action, Salome's kissing of the lips of the dismembered prophet. As the moon comes out again and its beams strike this scene of corruption and horror, Herod gives the final command: "Murder that woman!" The soldiers rush toward the little princess and bury her under their shields.

For the musical realization of this story of oriental splendor and depravity, Strauss calls upon every musical and instrumental effect which his brilliant craftsmanship and fertile imagination can evoke. Unexpected modulations, scintillating orchestral timbres create effects which, to use his own expression, resemble the shimmer of changing taffeta. Strauss blandly writes passages involving unheard-of difficulties of execution. The orchestral score gives explicit directions for the execution of phrases that at first glance look impossible. Strauss tells the timpani player how to set up his drums so that his two hands can alternate in the playing of a figure the like of which has never before been entrusted to kettle drums:

In another famous passage, the doublebasses are instructed to squeeze the string tightly between thumb and forefinger while bowing with very short, sharp strokes. The aim is to produce a sound "resembling the suppressed, choked moaning of a woman."

Here and there, Strauss must have felt that his demands exceeded the limit of what could be considered reasonable. In several places, footnotes in the score specify that if a player is unable to execute the notes, they are to be allotted to another instrumentalist or even omitted altogether!

No means are considered too grandiose or too cumbersome if a special effect is to be achieved. When, during her contemplation of Jokanaan's head, Salome says, "when I gazed upon you I heard mysterious music," a low A natural seems to appear from nowhere. This mysterious note actually comes from back stage, where it is played on a pipe organ, an effect used once again when Salome finally kisses Jokanaan's lips. Here the organ plays a soft C sharp minor triad in the low register. This chord is now combined with another clashing chord in the orchestra. The resulting dissonance illustrates Salome's words: "Ah, I have kissed your mouth, Jokanaan . . . there was a bitter taste on your lips . . . was it the taste of blood? . . . No, perhaps it tasted of love? . . . "

This bitter taste of blood and love permeates the whole opera. Nothing is more horrifyingly brutal than the scene of Narraboth's suicide. Salome has fallen in love with the prophet and after ecstatically praising the whiteness of his body and the splendor of his black hair, she finally decides that it is his mouth, the redness of his lips, that are the sum total of her desire! She extols the beauty of his mouth and the imagery of her passion becomes more and more daring. "The red fanfares of trumpets that announce the arrival of kings and frighten the enemy are not so red as your lips!" she says. Needless to say, these fanfares are dutifully illustrated in the orchestra:

Finally, Salome's passion culminates in one all-consuming yearning: "I want to kiss your mouth, Jokanaan! I want to kiss your mouth!"

ICH WILL DEINEN MUND KÜSSEN JO-KA-NA-AN

At this point, young Narraboth who is himself desperately in love with Salome, can no longer endure listening to these entreaties of love. "Princess, Princess," he begs, "you, who are like a garden of myrrh, who are like the dove of all doves, do not look at this man . . . do not speak such words to him . . . I cannot bear to hear them!" But Salome pays no attention to him. "I want to

261

kiss your mouth, Jokanaan," she continues to implore, and the phrase mounts higher up the scale:

ICH WILL DEINEN MUND KÜSSEN JO-KA-NA-AN

The tension of the scene now reaches its highest point, as Narraboth, in a desperate attempt to stop Salome, stabs himself and falls between the princess and the prophet. But she does not even notice the death of the man who adored her more than life itself. Ignoring completely the dead body, like one possessed, she keeps on with her *idée fixe*, pitching her plea still higher:

LASS MICH DEINEN MUND —— KÜSS —
-SEN, JO —KA— NA -AN. ——

Today, with our musical senses attuned to the idioms which Richard Strauss anticipated and matured with an objective appreciation for his style, we are able to respond to "Salome" as a work of art. The horrors fall into the background before the surpassing beauty of its musical language. Like any great artwork, "Oedipus Rex," "The Last Judgment," "Les Fleurs du Mal," the lurid details are submerged in a flood of magnificence. Art has invested horror with essential beauty.

Oscar Wilde's play "Salome" (1894) created more of a sensation in Germany than in France, where it had originally been conceived as a vehicle for Sarah Bernhardt. Its German translation, by Hedwig Lachmann, appealed so strongly to Richard Strauss that he accepted it as a libretto with only a few brief excisions and wrote music to accent and even exaggerate its essential qualities.

The première took place at the Royal Opera in Dresden on December 9, 1905, with Marie Wittich in the title role. Karl Burrian created an extraordinary portrayal of Herod, and he repeated it thirteen months later at the Metropolitan. Karl Perron was the first Jokanaan and Irene von Chavanne the first Herodias. Other members of the cast under Ernst von Schuch's baton were Riza Eibenschütz (Page of Herodias), Marie Keldorfer (Slave), Messrs. Plaschke and Kruis (Nazarenes), Jäger (Narraboth), Wachter (Cappadocian), Messrs. Nebuschka and Erwin (Soldiers), and the Messrs. Rüdiger, Salville, Grosch, Erl, and Rains (Five Jews).

A violent tempest of disapproval greeted "Salome" when Heinrich Conried, the general manager, introduced it on the Metropolitan Opera House stage on January 22, 1907, as a benefit for himself. After the première, which was paired with an instrumental and vocal concert and had been preceded by a general rehearsal the previous Sunday, the Board of Directors of the Metropolitan Opera and Real Estate Company which owned the theater decreed that "Salome" was "objectionable and detrimental to the best interests of the Metropolitan Opera House." In spite of Conried's petitions to restrict it to non-subscription performances or move it to another theater, the work was withdrawn.

"A sleek tigress with seduction speaking in every pose, gesture, look and utterance" to Henry Krehbiel of the Tribune, Olive Fremstad was acclaimed by this reviewer for accomplishing "a miracle." The Dance of the Seven Veils was performed for her by Bianca Froelich. Karl Burrian repeated his delineation of the "neurasthenic voluptuary," Herod "with amazing skill," Anton Van Rooy was given credit for the "prophetic breadth, dignity, and impressiveness" of his Jokanaan and Andreas Dippel's young Narraboth was called "an effective representation," by the Tribune reviewer. Richard Aldrich gave lavish praise in the Times to the conducting of Alfred Hertz.

Other members of the cast were Marion Weed (Herodias), Marie Mattfeld (Slave), Josephine Jacoby (Page), and Paul Lange (Cappadocian). Marcel Journet and Franz Stiner were the Nazarenes; Adolf Mühlmann and Robert Blass, Soldiers, and Albert Reiss, Julius Bayer, Giovanni Paroli, Jacques Bars, and Eugene Dufriche, the five Jews.

TANNHÄUSER

Whenever opera lovers get together one question is bound to come up: is the Golden Age of opera a thing of the past? There are always those who will smile sadly, shake their heads and declare: "Ah, there were giants in those days, and those days are gone forever!"

The truth of the matter is that it is extremely difficult to determine how the voices of the great singers of the past would compare with those of today, since there is no way of hearing the old and the new side by side. Recordings give us some impression of the singers of the not too distant past, but those early recordings, with their mechanical limitations, cannot give us a true picture. Modern electronic recording is of very recent vintage, while many of the greatest artists in the history of singing lived well before the birth of even the most primitive phonograph. As a result, to judge the voices of the past, we have to depend on recollections, memories, or even on pure hearsay—in other words, on notoriously unreliable evidence.

Distance always lends enchantment, and the passage of time has a way of cloaking our youthful musical experience in a golden and quite unrealistic haze!

We do possess plenty of concrete evidence, however, that all was not perfect even in the old days. Indeed, we need look no further than Wagner's own experiences in preparing the first production of "Tannhäuser" to see what operatic progress has been made since that day.

265

Wagner himself must be given credit for much of the progress. For one thing, he revolutionized the behaviour of the chorus. In the old days, the choristers are said to have marched on stage together, walked around in military fashion, and then placed themselves in rigid formation on either side. When they had sung the music allotted to them, they would re-form their column and stalk off in much the same way in which they had made their entrance!

Wagner insisted on something quite different: he broke the chorus up into small, individualized groups and made them participate fully in the dramatic action. The music he wrote for the different groups suggests exactly how he wanted a given scene to be staged.

The grand march in the second act, the entrance into the Hall of Song, demonstrates the composer's intentions clearly. Wagner makes of it a social occasion, not a military formation. The guests enter the throne room in small informal groups which the Landgrave and Elisabeth greet with friendly intimacy.

The details of the staging are clearly indicated as Wagner establishes the musical foundation for a charming and varied scenic picture.

Some sections of the march are noble and restrained, some are pompous and majestic, some have a light-hearted gaiety.

The various groups of guests conform to the character of their music; there is even a particularly delightful episode when some of the younger girls make their entrance and greet Elisabeth with adolescent enthusiasm.

Nowadays, we have a right to expect that kind of intelligent, imaginative musical staging, but it was quite revolutionary in Wagner's time. And it was by no means easy for Wagner to overcome the resistance of his colleagues in the field of stage

266

direction. On one occasion, when watching a rehearsal of the Entrance March, Wagner suggested sarcastically to the director that if he insisted on the stiff and senseless behavior of the chorus he should substitute the music of some other composer at this point!

The chorus of the Metropolitan Opera represents a great advance over the old days. Not only are the choristers thoroughly familiar with the music and staging of over thirty operas, sung in four different languages, but, at the same time, they have to learn new and different works, such as Britten's "Peter Grimes" or Stravinsky's "The Rake's Progress."

One aspect of the demands made on the chorus is that they are required to sing different characters in different acts of the same opera. Few people realize that this requires real acting ability. For example, the tenors and basses in the first and last act of "Tannhäuser" appear as penitent pilgrims, but in the second act, in different costumes of course, those same singers must portray noble knights!

The choristers were not the only wooden actors in Wagner's time. He experienced the same difficulty with many of his solo singers. Certain musical cuts in the first production of "Tannhäuser" were made necessary by the acting deficiencies of the performers. It must have been bitter for Wagner, who loved his scores and hated to sacrifice even a single note, to have to make cuts in Elisabeth's part, especially since the original portrayer of the role was his own niece and from all accounts a splendid vocalist. Nevertheless, the composer had to shorten her prayer to the Virgin in the third act and omit the important orchestral postlude which follows it entirely because the singer seemed unable to act it convincingly! Music and action are interdependent, the one geared to the other, as Wagner explicitly directs at this point.

267

At the conclusion of the prayer there is an extended scene during which Elisabeth does not sing a single note but expresses her thoughts in pantomime. She remains for a time completely absorbed, then rises slowly. She perceives Wolfram, who appears eager to approach her. She makes a gesture, indicating that she does not want him to speak to her. She again signifies that, although she is grateful from the depths of her heart for his faithful devotion, her way leads to Heaven, where she has a higher task to fulfill. She must go alone. She proceeds up the hill and gradually disappears on the path that leads to the castle.

Incredible as it may seem, Wagner had to delete this entire episode at the first performance because in rehearsal the singer made it so dull that the pantomime was completely meaningless.

Many of Wagner's male singers were equally obtuse! The eminent tenor Tichatschek, to whom the role of Tannhäuser was entrusted at the first performance, had a fine, ringing voice, but gave a simply ludicrous dramatic performance. Apparently he could sing only gay and brilliant music, and emotional depth was quite beyond him.

In spite of all Wagner's efforts, Tichatschek could not understand the dramatic significance of the character of Tannhäuser. In the contest scene in the Hall of Song, for example, Tannhäuser is supposed to forget his highly respectable surroundings and return in spirit to Venus and sensual love. When Tichatschek sang this invocation to Venus, he actually turned toward Elisabeth and poured his unholy raptures into *her* chaste ears! The singer's mental processes were very simple. Was he not the leading tenor, and was not Elisabeth the leading lady? To whom then, if not to the leading lady, should the tenor address himself at his big moment?

Today, of course, the integration of stage movement with the music is part of the stock-in-trade of every opera singer, but in

Wagner's time it was a new technique which owed its development to the master himself. Wagner's demand for a new and higher standard of artistic competence on the part of his singers developed a new school of singing-actors. Almost singlehanded, Wagner led the crusade against meaningless routine and initiated many reforms to which both the singers and audiences of today are the grateful heirs.

Two independent legends account for the story of "Tannhäuser." One is concerned with the Tournament of Music which was held by the Landgrave Hermann of Thuringia and his consort Sophie in 1206 at the Wartburg, a castle in the Bohemian mountains. The story of the festival, in which Walther von der Vogelweide, Wolfram von Eschenbach, Biterolf, and Heinrich von Ofterdingen participated, came to the attention of Richard Wagner in the stories of Ludwig Tieck and E. T. A. Hoffmann, which he read as a lonely young musician in Paris during the period 1839-1842. The other legend relates to the historical *Minnesinger* Tannhäuser, who flourished in the German courts from 1220-1250 and whose militant support of the Hohenstaufen dynasty caused the anathema of Pope Urban IV.

Identifying Tannhäuser with Heinrich von Ofterdingen, Wagner combined the legends into a single scenario. This he wrote in late June and July, 1842, while spending a brief vacation in Teplitz, near Dresden, and the Wostrai peak on the adjacent Schreckenstein, where he is said to have noted the song of a goatherd. The following May the libretto was completed, and in July the thirty-year-old composer was given a holiday by the management of the Dresden Opera to compose the music. The first act was written between July 1843, and January, 1844. The second act was composed in six weeks, concluded by October 15, 1844; the third act on December 29, 1844. Wagner finished the orchestra by April 15, 1845.

The composer himself conducted the première at the Royal Opera House in Dresden on October 19, 1845. Wilhelmine Schroeder-Devrient, who had also created the roles of Adriano Colonna in "Rienzi" and Senta in "The Flying Dutchman," was the Venus. Her friend Joseph Aloys Tichatschek was the Tannhäuser. Wagner's nineteen-year-old niece, Johanna Wagner, sang Elisabeth.

The baritone Mitterwurzer, "though betraying the blankest incapacity at the first rehearsals," according to Ernest Newman, finally mastered the new conception of operatic line implicit in the role of Wolfram. Dettmer was the Landgrave. The other minnesingers were Schloss as Walther, Wächter as Biterolf, Gurth as Heinrich, and Risse as Reinmar. New scenery was ordered by General-Manager Lüttichau from the Paris artist Desplechin, but an old Hall of Song setting from Weber's "Oberon" was used.

Karl Bergmann, former conductor of the New York Philharmonic and the Arion Society, introduced "Tannhäuser" to the United States on April 4, 1859, at the Stadt Theater in New York. Mr. and Mrs. Hugo Pickaneser sang the roles of Tannhäuser and Venus. The Minnesingers were the Messrs. Lehmann (Wolfram), Lotti (Walther), Urchs (Biterolf), Bolton (Heinrich), Brandt (Reinmar). Graff was the Landgrave, and Mme. Sidenburg the Elisabeth.

"Tannhäuser" was chosen to open the second season of opera at the Metropolitan on November 17, 1884 and to inaugurate the brief artistic direction of Leopold Damrosch, who also conducted the performance. Anton Schott made his debut as Tannhäuser. Auguste Krauss, soon to marry the eminent Wagnerian conductor, Anton Seidl, was the Elisabeth. Anna Slach, later demoted to Gutrunes and Frasquitas, began a two-year contract as Venus. Josef Kögel sang the Landgrave, 'Anna Stern a Shepherd, and the minstrel knights were Emil Tiferro (Walther), Josef Miller (Biterolf), Adolf Robinson (Wolfram), Otto Kemlitz (Heinrich), and Ludwig Wolf (Reinmar).

TOSCA

O NE of the keenest judges of operatic librettos was Giacomo Puccini. Forever in search of suitable material, he scrutinized innumerable stories, plays, novels, and poems, and rejected hundreds of possibilities before he found a subject to satisfy him.

The composer has left us his own exposition of the criteria by which he judged a potential opera book. The perfect story for opera, he said, must be sympathetic, vibrant, full of life, emotion, vitality, sentiment, and humanity. Its universal human appeal he considered its most important characteristic, since only with emotion can enduring triumph be achieved.

Not every story with human appeal, however, proved appropriate to Puccini. He required dramatic elements suitable to the theater, elements which obeyed the fixed law of the stage: the necessity to interest, to surprise, to move.

Having selected the play or the novel which was to serve as the basis for his opera, Puccini supervised the work of his librettists with never-ending patience and with an unbending determination to get what he wanted. Everything they wrote was to be subordinate to one principle: the truthful presentation of the characters. Neither poetic nor musical considerations were allowed to interfere with this aim. Puccini would rather have one touching subtle truth than pages of "development."

His sense of economy, his dread of redundancy, are almost without parallel in the history of opera. In these days when we are so impatient with *longueurs,* when we want to streamline, to condense, to get it over with, Puccini's operas remain as they have always been, untampered with and uncut. Nobody has ever suggested the omission of a single tiny detail! Typical of this struggle for complete truthfulness in any given situation is the fact that in the original sketch for the libretto of "Tosca," Cavaradossi was to sing a solo aria while being tortured, and the voices of Tosca, the judge, and Spoletta were to join him later in a formal quartet. This conventional operatic technique was unacceptable to Puccini. At this point the dramatic situation, the human conflict, simply did not permit such a static musical treatment. The composer argued with his writers until they finally came up with the exciting dramatic scene we know.

Puccini's obsession with dramatic veracity has resulted in a strange and very unusual lack of instrumental music which can be transplanted to the concert hall. From the overtures of Gluck and Mozart to Siegfried's Rhine Journey, Salome's Dance, the "Rosenkavalier" Waltzes, and the Sea Interludes from "Peter Grimes," there is a never-ending wealth of operatic material which has acquired an independent life of its own. Nothing of the sort exists where Puccini is concerned. His operas contain no overtures, ballets, or instrumental *intermezzi* which could be transplanted to the concert stage. His music has no existence except as it relates to the play; it is never allowed to stroll away and enjoy a little excursion of its own. Its only purpose is to vitalize and enhance the theatrical happenings and to help the characters of the drama to project their feelings and actions more convincingly.

This desire for truthful detail is reflected not only in the absence of any music which is not justified by the dramatic situation; it also induces the composer to give an amazing amount of attention to the stage itself. In Puccini's operas not only do we see what is on the stage but we are fully informed of what

273

is located in the neighborhood of the immediate visible area. In the second act of "Tosca" we see Scarpia's room in the Palazzo Farnese, but we are equally conscious of the surrounding territory. We know of the reception rooms outside. Through the open window we hear the distant strains of an old-fashioned gavotte. Victory is being celebrated in an unseen ball-room, while a devout cantata is sung in gratitude. We are likewise aware of the torture chamber next to Scarpia's room on one side of the stage and of the courtyard on the other side where the snare drums accompany Cavaradossi to his prison cell. We know where all these doors and windows lead, and we have the feeling that the actors are human beings who continue to live in these other spaces rather than singers who proceed to their dressing rooms to take off their wigs and costumes.

And in the last act we get a very definite idea of the location of the Castel Sant'Angelo when we hear a dozen of Rome's churches sound their matins from various directions, and when outside, by the shores of the Tiber, the shepherd leads his flock and we hear not only his melancholy song but also the little bells tied around the necks of his sheep.

A few years ago a critic remarked that the operas of Puccini— and he singled out "Tosca" for special mention—were unthinkable without the Wagnerian heritage of leading motives. This is undoubtedly true, but it is important to note that, while Wagner weaves most of his musical fabric out of his motives, Puccini uses them more sparingly and only in order to make a special dramatic point.

In the very opening phrase of "Tosca" Puccini introduces a ⌐⌐ccession of three chords which thereafter are associated with t⌐ ⁁ villainous chief of police, Scarpia, that "bigoted lecher and hy⌐ocrite, secretly steeped in vice, though outwardly pious," as Ca⌐aradossi describes him.

When Tosca kills Scarpia at the end of the second act, his musical theme undergoes a subtle transformation. The succession of three chords remains, but the last chord appears in the minor mode, almost as if it had been deprived of its vicious sting!

Even though Scarpia is dead, his spirit lingers on long enough to fulfill his nefarious plotting. When the last act opens we see the starlit Roman sky, whose transparency is conveyed in musical terms as the chill of the night spreads through the scene before the dawn breaks. It is only when Scarpia's theme is insinuated into this cool and beautiful atmosphere that we begin to suspect that his vengeance will continue.

275

It is Scarpia's ghost that stalks the Roman night!

Puccini is fond of converting the important melodies of his arias and duets into motives to be used later when the composer wants to refer to the situation which called forth the melody in the first place. The melody which Cavaradossi sings in the first act, when he tries to appease Tosca's jealousy, returns with great dramatic effect in the second act. This might be called the motive of Tosca as she appears in the eyes of Cavaradossi when he sings the praises of Tosca's lustrous dark eyes.

In the second act, when Tosca encounters Cavaradossi in Scarpia's apartments in the palace, this theme makes a dramatic reappearance. Tosca knows that her suspicions had been groundless, but jealousy has done its work: she has led Scarpia's agents to the hidden fugitive. As Tosca appears we hear this theme, while Cavaradossi hurriedly warns her to say nothing of what she has seen at the villa.

At this point Cavaradossi is taken out to be tortured. Later, when he is brought back in a state of collapse, we again hear Tosca's theme:

The first act love duet provides another example of this "melody into leading motive" technique, for it shows up in both the second and the third acts. We hear it in its extended form in the first act, as Tosca admits her jealousy and Cavaradossi repeats his protestations of undying love.

This theme becomes, in effect, Cavaradossi's last memory of Tosca. Puccini makes a dramatic point by bringing the theme back in the final act when Cavaradossi is permitted to write a last letter to Tosca before his execution. He sits down to write, lost in thought, and we hear Cavaradossi remembering fondly other nights when Tosca came through the garden of his little villa.

Puccini's use of a leading motive can reveal a character's secret thoughts even when he is talking about something else, as in Cavaradossi's concern for Angelotti when he is supposed to be thinking only of his rendezvous with Tosca. Angelotti, the

278

political fugitive, is established with a theme of his own at the very opening of the opera.

Later, in the first act, when Tosca is planning the love meeting at Cavaradossi's villa, he answers her somewhat absentmindedly: "Tonight?" As the music tells us, his real concern at the moment is about Angelotti:

In opera *men* may lie, but music . . . never! Or, at least, not music from the pen of that master of our own century, the man who never fails to touch the listening heart and completely satisfy the logic of the mind: Giacomo Puccini.

The composer Giacomo Puccini was first drawn to the subject of Tosca, when he saw Sarah Bernhardt, who had created the title role of Victorien Sardou's play in Paris in 1887, perform it in Florence. Two years later, he wrote his publisher Giulio Ricordi and asked him to obtain the author's permission. Puccini lost interest for a while, but in 1895 he again considered the subject. In the intervening period, the composer Alberto Franchetti had become interested in the Sardou play and even had a libretto written by Luigi Illica (1857-1912). The wily Ricordi persuaded Franchetti to relinquish his rights. Illica and his colleague, Giuseppe Giacosa, discarding most of the political complications in favor of romantic melodrama, revised the embryonic libretto so successfully that the playwright, Sardou, (1831-1908) admitted it was an improvement over the original play.

To provide the right atmosphere for composition, Puccini chose a tiny mountain village called Chiatri, where he escaped the heat of the plains and worked from 10 p.m. until 4 a.m. every day. Then he hurried to Paris for a visit with Sardou to discuss royalties, Tosca's death and the course of the River Tiber. The music occupied him from June, 1898, to September, 1899.

Remembering the original fiasco of "La Bohème," Puccini was nervous when he arrived in Rome for the première of "Tosca" on January 14, 1900. His conductor, Leopold Mugnone, was also troubled by the rumor of an impending disturbance. A bomb was even hinted at. The curtain rose, Angelotti entered, a murmur filled the Costanzi Theater, and the conductor promptly signalled to have the curtain lowered again.

Even with this false start, "Tosca" was a success from the first, in spite of the faint praise of the local critics. The beautiful Ericlea Darclée proved an excellent actress in the title role. Emilio De Marchi was the Cavaradossi, and Eugenio Giraldoni, the first Boris Godunov in France, was Scarpia. The rest of the cast included Enrico Galli (Angelotti), Ettore Borelli (Sacristan),

280

Enrico Giordani (Spoletta), Giuseppe Gironi (Sciarrone), Aristide Parasassi (Jailer), and Angelo Righi (Shepherd).

"Tosca" began its American career on February 4, 1901, at the Metropolitan, with a sumptuous scenic investiture which was praised both by the Times and Tribune critics. "The tragic power" disclosed by Milka Ternina in the title role was also noted by Mr. Krehbiel, but Antonio Scotti's Scarpia, which held the Metropolitan public spellbound for over thirty years, did not immediately receive the appreciation it deserved, although Mr. Henderson later called it "a brilliantly vigorous and aggressive impersonation." The rest of the cast under Luigi Mancinelli's conducting comprised Eugène Dufriche as Angelotti; Giuseppe Cremonini, rated only fair, as Cavaradossi; Charles Gilibert, the Sacristan; Jacques Bars, Spoletta; Lodovico Viviani, Sciarrone; and Cernusco, the Jailer.

LA TRAVIATA

ROM almost every angle "La Traviata" stands as an artistic creation of the highest order, but in no respect more than in the realm of character portrayal. Here is first and foremost a portrait, a living and growing likeness expressed in musical and dramatic terms. The whole story, its pathos and tragedy, seems to evolve directly from the character of Violetta. In no other work is the central figure so dominating, so responsible for the entire course of the action.

If Violetta were the shallow, frivolous sort of person she first appears, the story would not have developed as it does. But even before the curtain rises, the listener realizes from the orchestral prelude the complicated character of her nature.

The initial phrases entrusted to divided strings refer to the insidious illness which is undermining her health:

Then comes that intensely moving theme which symbolizes Violetta's capacity for sincere and profound devotion, for the kind of love of which she at first thinks herself incapable:

282

Why she believes this also becomes apparent as that love theme is combined with the light-hearted ornamentations and frivolous arabesques depicting the laughter of the professional courtesan:

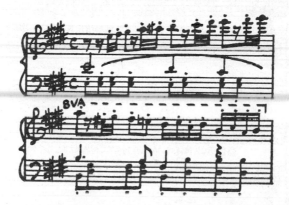

During most of the first act, Violetta's music is dominated by this shallow glitter of the decadent salons: She quite candidly advises Alfredo to forget her since she would be unable to return such serious, or, as she puts it, "such heroic" love!

But even in the first act we begin to witness a strange transformation of Violetta's attitude, and it is very significant that
this change is brought about by Alfredo's ardent declaration of
love, which is couched in a melody which bears an astonishing
resemblance to her own love theme.

In her first act aria, Violetta repeats Alfredo's melody, and one
cannot escape the conclusion that it was the sincerity of his

284

feelings that made her aware of her own innermost emotional resources.

These two melodies, Alfredo's declaration and Violetta's love theme which we heard in the prelude, are so similar in construction that one seems to be a variation of the other, or, shall we say, its perfect musical complement. The romantic conception of one individual depending on the other and existing as the chief reason for the other's being is clearly expressed in the music. Both melodies are built around the descending scale, and in both the climax occurs on the same high note. One is full of a typically masculine verve and energy, the other is feminine and passive, but in their basic sameness lies the subtle revelation that here are two individuals destined for each other, and that Violetta, even while pursuing her life of shallow pleasure, is ready and waiting for the great love Alfredo has to offer.

In the second act, in the monumental scene with Alfredo's father, we meet a different Violetta, a woman fighting for her happiness, a woman unwilling to give up her new-found love for any but the supreme reason—her lover's enduring happiness. In agitated, breathless sentences she tries to convince the older Germont that Alfredo means everything to her. She has no family, no friends, and there remains for her only a short span of life.

When Violetta finally agrees to Germont's demands, it is only because she realizes that society will never forgive her, and that she could only be a hopeless burden to Alfredo, a tragic obstacle for the young man's chances for success and happiness. It is then that she sings that unforgettable sentence which reveals the very essence of her unhappy fate: "A woman, once fallen, can never rise again . . . and even though the good Lord may take pity on her, the world will never forgive her!"

But how can she ever convince Alfredo that they should separate? His father's arguments would never make any impression on him; if anything, they would only make him more positive in his devotion to her! And so Violetta decides to use extraordinary measures: she decides to make Alfredo hate her. The letter she writes him telling him of her decision to return to her former life of luxury and pleasure is one of the most heartbreaking messages ever penned by a woman. It is Verdi's everlasting glory that he found the unique clarinet melody to accompany Violetta's writing of the fateful letter.

Then, in the final farewell to Alfredo, she pours out all her heart, and we finally hear that passionate love theme of the prelude sung by Violetta herself:

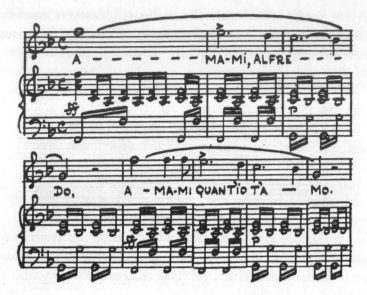

Everything that follows—the humiliation and suffering of her encounter with Alfredo at Flora's party, the aggravation of her long illness, the long weeks and months of waiting for death and perhaps for Alfredo's return—all this is the inevitable result of her supreme sacrifice.

In the last act, chastened by suffering, Violetta gives eloquent testimony of the self-control she has attained. As the heroine offers Alfredo her picture and asks him to give it to whomever he marries, the melodic line of her singing seems serene and undisturbed. Yet at the same time the orchestra, punctuating her words with mighty chords, betrays the heartrending agony of her true feelings:

It is this clarity, this keen musical perception with which Verdi applied perspective and color to his heroine, that enables the singing actress to make the character her own.

The role of Violetta is one of the most demanding in the repertory. The soprano never leaves the stage during acts I and IV, and there are only short periods during the middle acts when she can catch a breath and relax offstage. More than four-fifths of the time that the curtain is up she is there before us, acting and singing! But to the extent that she can subordinate her personality to Verdi's melodic and orchestral subtleties, she will give the spectator the illusion that the music is but the shadow of herself.

In his concentration on "the lady of the camellias," Verdi made her live through any artist who approaches her with perfect command of vocal, musical, and stage techniques. For, in the last analysis, it is Verdi's music which recreates her for us today.

289

〰〰〰〰〰〰〰

Giuseppe Verdi attended Alexandre Dumas' play, "La Dame aux Camélias," in Paris early in 1852 and studied the text during the following autumn. The libretto was not completed by Francesco Piave until after January, 1853, and the music was composed rapidly, some of it on shipboard between Genoa and Civitavecchia, some of it during the rehearsals of "Il Trovatore." Verdi himself conducted the première at the Fenice Theater in Venice, on March 6, 1853. The opera was at first a failure partly because of the inability of the public to accept a realistic subject in modern dress, partly because of the ample proportions and mature appearance of the Violetta, Fanny Salvini-Donatelli. Lodovico Graziani sang Alfredo and was later rewarded for his talents by a contract at La Scala. Felice Varesi was Giorgio Germont, the remainder of the cast being Carlotta Berini (Annina), Dragone (Douphol), Zuliani (Gastone), Silvestri (d'Obigny), Bellini (Grenvil), and Speranza (Flora).

In spite of the disapproval of Queen Victoria and squeamish European critics, "La Traviata" was received by an enthusiastic public and a divided press in New York when it was first presented at the Academy of Music on December 3, 1856 by the McMahon-Strakosch Company. The Post considered that Anna de LaGrange sang "admirably well (as Violetta) with her well-known truth and brilliancy." The Herald critic said that Pasquale Brignoli "appeared to great advantage" as Alfredo, and the Times noted that Signor Amodio "sang delicately and well" as Germont. Mme. Siedenburg was the Flora and Max Maretzek conducted.

"La Traviata" was introduced under Auguste Vianesi's baton

to the Metropolitan Opera public on November 5, 1883, with Marcella Sembrich in the title role at the age of twenty-five. Victor Capoul, adored by the ladies for his exquisite art and fetching bang, sang Alfredo, and the popular Neapolitan baritone, Giuseppe Del Puente, was Germont. Other roles were assigned to Achille Augier (Douphol), Vincenzo Fornaris (Gastone), Baldassare Corsi (d'Obigny), Ludovico Contini (Grenvil), Emily Lablache (Flora), and Imogene Forti (Annina).

TRISTAN UND ISOLDE

A NOTEWORTHY feature of "Tristan und Isolde" is that the tragic story is well under way when the curtain rises on the first act and many important events have already taken place. Wagner, in fashioning his own version of the story from the many varying "Tristan and Isolde" legends, chose to begin at a point where the tragedy is close to its final climax. Thus, to approach this opera without some knowledge of what has gone before, is much like hurrying to the last, climactic chapter of a story without bothering to read a synopsis of previous chapters.

Of course Wagner makes frequent allusions in his text to these previous occurrences. You hear much concerning what has happened in the past, even if you neglected to do your homework. And yet, unless you follow the text word-for-word, you could entirely miss this exposition of past events.

So, since a real understanding of "Tristan" depends on the knowledge of what has taken place before the opera, let us try to reconstruct these earlier events of the story.

We know that the Irish princess, Isolde, had been engaged to a nobleman and warrior of her own land, Morold. She says as much to Tristan, near the end of the first act. "He was betrothed to me, that noble Irish hero," Isolde sings, "I had put my blessing on his weapons, and it was for me that he fought."

We know, too, that Morold had set out with his army to collect the yearly tribute which the rebellious King Marke of Cornwall had refused to pay. Morold was then defeated in battle by King Marke's nephew, Tristan, who, instead of paying tribute, defiantly sent Morold's severed head back to Ireland. Kurvenal tells us of this in the first act, obviously relishing the grisly details: "Morold crossed the sea to collect the Cornish tax. But now he lies buried on a deserted island, and his head hangs in Ireland as a tax paid by England."

Tristan, however, did not escape unscathed from his encounter with Morold, and, to make matters worse, his wounds had refused to heal. Knowing of Isolde's prowess with curative herbs and medicinal potions, he embarked for Ireland disguised as a lonely seaman calling himself Tantris. We learn this from Isolde's own lips early in the first act: "A boat came to the Irish coast," she tells her maid, Brangäne. "In it a dying man . . . he knew of my skill, and I treated his wounds faithfully."

Isolde recognizes him as Tristan because a fragment lodged in the head of the slain Morold matches exactly a dent in Tristan's sword. Here was Isolde's opportunity if she wanted revenge: sword in hand, she stood over her helpless enemy— but he looked up, their eyes met, and she was unable to act. The theme of the glance, representing the moment when Tristan and Isolde fell in love, is of crucial importance and is heard throughout the opera.

No words were exchanged, and the secret of that love was buried deep within their breasts.

Cured, Tristan returns to Cornwall, but the image of the beauteous Irish princess keeps haunting his mind. In the meantime his enemies at home, envious of his achievements, accuse him of being overly ambitious, of aiming to succeed to the throne of his uncle, King Marke. Tristan therefore considers it a point of honor to urge his uncle to marry, and praises Isolde far and wide as the only maiden worthy to be queen. Tristan even threatens to leave Marke's court forever unless the King consents to woo Isolde. Finally the monarch consents and sends

293

Tristan to Ireland as "bridebearer." This information is conveyed to the listeners during the second act duet between Tristan and Isolde as well as in King Marke's monologue near the end of that act.

Tristan's mission to Ireland on the king's behalf is certainly far from complimentary to the fair Isolde. Not only is she a political pawn, being delivered, as she says, "like a corpse to her country's victorious enemies," but her emotions are further lacerated by the justifiable fury of a woman scorned. Such is the state of events when the curtain opens on the first act of the opera.

Isolde is enraged to the point where she actually calls upon the storms to arise and destroy the ship and every being on it. Later in the first act she specifically calls down curses on Tristan's head. She seems to realize the fateful nature of their relationship, as she must have known it earlier when she put down her sword and allowed Tristan and their love to survive. "A curse upon you, the betrayer!" she sings. "A curse upon your head. Revenge! Death for us both!"

Tristan himself is far from happy in the situation to which his sense of honor has led him. In the first act, when the two lovers finally meet at Isolde's insistence, Tristan, stung anew by her violent reproaches, hands her his sword and stands ready to let her kill him then and there. In this tortured, frantic state of mind the two lovers finally drink the love potion. As far as Tristan and Isolde are concerned, they are concluding a suicide pact. This is indicated by the themes of the death potion and of death itself. "For the deepest agony, for the greatest suffering, there is only one remedy: the drink of death."

Tristan is just as convinced as Isolde that it is poison they are taking. He refers to it as "the drink of oblivion." Both are

294

quite ready to die, since life in this situation seems unbearable to them.

It is only now, when the two lovers think themselves on the brink of death, or, as Wagner puts it, "when the gates of death open before them," that they confess their love to each other. All worldly considerations of honor, propriety, and convention vanish into thin air. "Tristan . . . Isolde . . . beloved," they murmur, completely oblivious of the bustling activity going on around them as the ship prepares to land.

The precise contents of the drink are not of any real importance. They might just as well have drunk water. What this drinking of the potion represents is the moment of their mutual avowal. It is significant that the potion, which was to have brought instant death, set them upon an apparently different path, the path of passionate love, although this path brings them ultimately to the same goal. Death was merely delayed!

When Wagner wrote "Tristan," he was under the spell of that archpessimist among philosophers, Arthur Schopenhauer. Hence this idealization of death as the one great reality is a recurrent note throughout this opera. From the moment of the declaration of their love, Tristan and Isolde live in another world indeed, in the realm of death, of "night," as Wagner calls it. Death has become an obsession with them. The second act love duet is full of repeated references to the dreaded, treacherous world of "day," in contrast to the welcome oblivion of "night."

Although Wagner's philosophical slant is clearly spelled out in the text, most listeners still interpret the story as a normal and more or less conventional love affair involving the usual triangle of husband, wife and lover. As a matter of fact, it is not surprising that the metaphysical implications of the score should so often be overlooked. Music does not lend itself too well to the portrayal of abstract ideas. Its strength lies rather in ap-

295

pealing to our emotions. The music of "Tristan" is love music of agonizing beauty and provides an overwhelming emotional experience, for it is the musical embodiment of our conception of romantic love. We have all grown up with our ideals of love dominated by that conception, since it is part of our civilization.

The "Tristan and Isolde" myth, clothed in this ineffably beautiful music, can therefore evoke an intensely personal reaction on the part of the listener. To each of us it represents his own story, for it follows a familiar pattern of human emotional behavior. Isolde, resisting and hesitating, clinging to childhood, security and protection, fights love because to yield will lead to death. Tristan struggles against his allegiance to King Marke, the symbol of authority and paternity. Ultimately both must yield to the dictates of their overmastering need for love.

Richard Wagner first mentioned the possibility of an opera on the Tristan legend in a letter to Franz Liszt in December, 1854. Well-acquainted with Gottfried von Strassburg's version of the Twelfth-Century poem, Wagner turned to the subject as one which was suitable for a practicable stage work with only five principal singers, a less exacting problem than the epic "Ring" on which he was working at the time.

Toward the end of April, 1857, he drafted a scenario for "Tristan" and completed the poem on September 18, presenting it to Mathilde Wesendonck, who is said to have inspired its composition.

The musical sketch was started October 1, the first act completed by New Year's, and the second act the following July. Meanwhile Wagner began the orchestral sketch of the first act on November 5, 1857, finishing it by January 13 and turning to the second act as soon as the sketch was completed. He and his wife Minna were living in the Asyl, a guest-house of the Wesendonck family on their estate near Zurich, at this time, a period melodramatically interrupted by Mme. Wagner's rebellion at her husband's romantic attachment to his patron's wife.

In September, 1858, Wagner rented a suite of rooms in the Giustiani Palace in Venice, where he composed the second act in comparative peace. In March, 1859, however, he was advised by the Venetian authorities to withdraw, and decided to settle in Lucerne. There he began the third act on April 9, completing the orchestration the following July.

In 1860 "Tristan" was pronounced "unproduceable" by the authorities in Karlsruhe. During the following year the composer visited Vienna, where "Tristan" had been accepted for production, but the work was abandoned after seventy-seven rehearsals.

The patronage of the enthusiastic young King Ludwig II of Bavaria finally brought about the première of "Tristan" in the Royal Court Theater in Munich on June 10, 1865, six years after the last note had been written. The title roles were taken by Malvina Garrigues, whose sudden hoarseness had caused a last-minute postponement from the original date, May 15, and her young husband, Ludwig Schnorr von Carolsfeld. The tenor, a fine interpreter of Wagner's hero, died of a sudden apoplectic attack ten days after the première, having sung only three performances of "Tristan." Mitterwurzer, the original Wolfram, "occasionally overacted" as Kurvenal, according to Newman, and Zottmayer, the King Marke, struck the nervous conductor Hans von Bülow, as "weak in the head but strong in the lungs."

297

Anna Deinet, later married to the famous actor, Ernst von Possart, was judged "very capable" as Brangäne. Heinrich sang Melot; Simons, the Shepherd, and Hartmann, the Helmsman. Anton Seidl, who introduced "Tristan und Isolde" to this country on December 1, 1886, assembled a great cast under his baton at the Metropolitan Opera House. Albert Niemann, the Tristan, although fifty-five at the time, was hailed by Henry Krehbiel in the Tribune for "the plastic dignity and beauty" of his attitudes and the "vitalizing power" of his declamation. The passionate intensity of Lilli Lehmann, then at the height of her career, was considered ideally fitting Isolde, and Marianne Brandt was commended for her sincerity as Brangäne and Adolf Robinson for his tenderness as Kurvenal. Emil Fischer's King Marke was judged "musically excellent." Max Alvary, a renowned Tristan of eight years later, sang the Sailor; Rudolf von Milde, the first Metropolitan Alberich, was Melot; Otto Kemlitz, a popular David and Mime, the Shepherd; and Emil Sänger, the Helmsman.

IL TROVATORE

OPERA was born in Italy, and to the Italians it is the most natural form of musical expression. It is only natural that the atmosphere of Italian operatic music should take its character from the temperament of the Italian people. When we try to analyze this atmosphere, we find something which might be best described as "excitement."

When opera was in its infancy, Claudio Monteverdi, the most important of the Italian pioneers on the opera stage, developed a style of music he called *"lo stile concitato,"* "the excited style," and the history of Italian opera from Monteverdi to the present day is in a sense a history of the development of this excited style.

The Italians have succeeded in creating and sustaining such a high degree of intensity as the basis of their operas that the great German philosopher, Friedrich Nietzsche, referred to it as the "Mediterranean" quality in music.

No composer has put more of this hot-blooded passion into his music than Giuseppe Verdi, and in none of Verdi's operas do we find more intensity, more emotional energy and fire than in "Il Trovatore." As we look at the four leading characters, Leonora, Manrico, Azucena and the Count, we find that each one of them is called on to deliver musical passages of almost insane ferocity or ecstatic rapture.

Verdi had a special fondness for dramatic situations which were breathlessly exciting. This very breathlessness he projected into his melodic line by cutting it into short bits to express the frenzy of his characters' feelings.

299

In the second act, for example, Leonora is astounded and overjoyed to find Manrico at her side when she had supposed him to be dead. "Do my eyes deceive me?" she sings. "Are you there beside me, or is it a dream? My heart is almost bursting with joy!"

In the last act, frantic with worry, she pleads with the Count to spare Manrico's life. "Have pity, have pity," she begs, in wild agitation.

A little later Leonora is breathless again, this time with joy,
as the Count, in exchange for her promise of marriage, gives
the order to spare Manrico's life. "He will live," she exclaims.
"My heart throbs indescribably."

Verdi's characters are constantly assuring us that the state of their emotions defies description, and then they proceed to describe it with the utmost vividness, aided and abetted by the music. It is remarkable, with the rapid pulse and high blood pressure which is apparently their normal state, that they manage to survive at all.

And yet it is this very state of perpetual excitement which gives rise to the composer's finest pages. The insane ravings and wild hallucinations of Azucena find eloquence in great melodies each time she relives the agonizing moment when she saw her mother being burned at the stake.

"Look," she cries in the last act, "see how the flames writhe round her body like snakes . . . her white hair blazes into flame . . . her tortured eyes stare from their sockets."

The finale of the last act piles one burst of emotional excitement on another. Manrico is horrified by the suspicion that his life has been saved at the price of Leonora's yielding to the Count. His blood pressure rises several notches higher:

Then Leonora pleads with him to flee while there is still time to save his life. She urges him frantically and finally confesses breathlessly that, rather than marry the Count, she has taken poison.

It must be apparent from even these few examples that to do justice to Verdi's feverish music the singer must be able not only to sing such passages in a technically correct manner but to give them their full emotional intensity.

The popular misconception of the so-called artistic temperament suggests the prima-donna fighting over curtain calls, or going into hysterics if the impresario won't take her dog out to walk. In other words temperament has been confused with plain bad temper and bad manners. Real artistic temperament is harder to define. It consists of vitality and energy of emotional expression; it is composed of imagination, insight, and the capacity to take fire within oneself and make the audience feel the heat of that fire.

Verdi prized this quality of temperament highly. He would often forgive lack of musicianship or clumsiness of appearance for the sake of genuine emotional fire.

The original Manrico in Rome was the tenor, Carlo Baucardé. In the famous third act aria, "Di quella pira," he had difficulties during rehearsals in hitting the G sharp:

The night of the performance he finally became so excited, so temperamental if you like, that instead of the G sharp he landed on a high C:

The audience was amazed and delighted and the note has since become a "must" for every Manrico to follow. Thus temperament triumphed over sober intelligence.

Although Verdi normally was adamant against changes, he seems to have approved this particular alteration. He knew that first and foremost the audience must be moved. That is why he valued temperament in his singers so highly. He was confident that, with singers of great emotional intensity, the blazing pages of "Il Trovatore" would never fail to achieve their effect.

The composer, Giuseppe Verdi, discussed the Spanish drama "El Trobador," written at the age of 23 by Antonio Gutierrez (1836), with his librettist, Salvatore Cammarano (1801-1852), early in 1851. Composition was interrupted by the death of Verdi's mother (June 13, 1851) and the illness of his father (March, 1852), but was completed in November, 1852. At the death of the librettist in July, 1852, Verdi called in the poet Leone

Emanuele (1820-1890) for final touches and sent an additional hundred ducats to Cammarano's widow. The première at the Apollo Theater in Rome on January 19, 1853, was threatened by an overflow of the Tiber but every seat was occupied. Its success was proved by the clamor of a capacity audience and by the acclaim of such critics as the Roman correspondent of the Gazzetta Musicale, who praised the "originality and exquisite artistry" of Azucena's enunciation.

The first Leonora was Rosina Penco. Her Manrico was the chubby-faced matinee idol, Carlo Baucardé. Mme. Goggi was the Azucena, Mme. Quadri the Inez. Giovanni Giucciardi the Count di Luna; Balderi the Ferrando, and Bazzoli the Ruiz.

Max Maretzek introduced "Il Trovatore" to this country on May 2, 1855, conducting a fine cast at the Academy of Music. Rina Steffanone, whose voice was said to have been made by nature for the portrayal of broken-hearted women, was Leonora. Amodio, huge in voice and girth, was the Count; while the popular tenor, Pasquale Brignoli, was described as warbling with his throat but wabbling on his legs. Felicita Vestvali was the Azucena; Rocco, the Ferrando, and Quinto, the Ruiz.

The third opera to reach the Metropolitan Opera stage, "Il Trovatore" was conducted by Auguste Vianesi on October 26, 1883, with Alwina Valleria (nee Schoening, from Baltimore) making her debut as Leonora. Even more important, on that occasion, was the debut, in the role of Azucena, of Zelia Trebelli, a mature Parisian mezzo-soprano, who was later the first Metropolitan Carmen. The handsome Sicilian tenor, Roberto Stagno, praised by Wagner for his Lohengrin was Manrico. Imogene Forti sang Inez; Emile Augier, Ferrando; and Amadeo Grazzi, Ruiz.